SPEAKING OUT:

THOUGHTS OF AN INDEPENDENT LIBERAL CONSERVATIVE CHRISTIAN TEACHER

FREDERICK WULFF

outskirtspress
DENVER, COLORADO

The opinions expressed in this manuscript are solely the opinions of the author and do not represent the opinions or thoughts of the publisher, or the persons (Tom and Matthew Spoden) pictured in photographs. The author has represented and warranted full ownership and/or legal right to publish all the materials in this book.

Speaking Out:
Thoughts Of An Independent Liberal Conservative Christian Teacher
All Rights Reserved.
Copyright © 2014 Frederick Wulff
v2.0

Cover Photo © 2014 JupiterImages Corporation. All rights reserved - used with permission.

This book may not be reproduced, transmitted, or stored in whole or in part by any means, including graphic, electronic, or mechanical without the express written consent of the publisher except in the case of brief quotations embodied in critical articles and reviews.

Outskirts Press, Inc.
http://www.outskirtspress.com

ISBN: 978-1-4787-2352-3

Outskirts Press and the "OP" logo are trademarks belonging to Outskirts Press, Inc.

PRINTED IN THE UNITED STATES OF AMERICA

CONTENTS

Introduction i

Chapter One: History And Teaching History 1
   Making Sense Out Of History: Food For Thought 1
      A Disturbing Trend: Disjointed History
      The Unraveling of History – The Loss of Cohesiveness
      The Fallacy: There Is Your Truth and There Is My Truth
      A Dilemma: Over-Compensation with "Cherry Picking"
      Examine The Whole Picture: Drink Deep or Taste Not
   Teaching Social Studies Without A Negative Paradigm 6
      Is the United States a Terrible Country?
      Needed Stress on a Positive Multiculturalism
      The Perversion of Multiculturalism
      Critical Thinking or a Negative Agenda?
      Responsible Instruction
      Current Events – History in the Making
      Conclusion
   Weakness In Social Studies Textbooks 13
      Second Class is Not Good Enough
      Weaknesses that Perpetuate Myths and Misconceptions in Specific Areas
      Weaknesses of Simple Errors
      The Weaknesses of Forced "Christian" History
      The Weaknesses of Omission and Fragmentation
      Epilogue
   A Good Social Studies Textbook 24
      The Bradley Commission Recommendations
      State Recommendations
      Scholarship

    The Textbook Author as Educator
    Treatment of Constitutional History
    Relating Geography to History
    Relating Religion to History
    The Treatment of Women and Minorities
    Creative Strategies
    The Time Element and Grade Placement
Movies As History 33
    Movies on Television
    Develop Historical Empathy
    Seek Historical Accuracy
    Be Informed
    Distorted History: Movies with an Agenda
    A Word to the Wise
    Sources for History Movie Reviews
Teaching Social Studies: The Controversy Over Standards 40
    Introduction: The Neglected Subject
    The Minnesota Standards: Lightning Rod for Controversy
    The Argument for Stress on Historical Content
    The Need for Critical Thinking in the Standards
    Standards that Promote Democratic Institutions
    The Ongoing Controversy and Politics
    Standards that Serve Students
Credit Where Credit Is Due: Talent In Our Midst 47
Remembering John Dickinson 48
    Countering an Unfavorable Image
    The Penman of the Revolution
    Christian Respect for Government
    Citing the Rights of Englishmen
    Formulator of the Articles of Confederation
    Contributions to the United States Constitution
    Supporting Ratification of the Constitution
Political Activism In The Organization Of American History.. 53

Chapter Two: Race And Multiculturalism 55
  Build Bridges to Other Cultures 55
    The Opportunities for Building Bridges
    Prepare for Bridge Building with the Word of God
    Develop Bridge Building Skills by Studying History
    Find Models of Bridge Builders in History
    Enhance Bridge Building by Personal Travel
    Use Bridge Building Class Assignments
    Build Bridges in Your Neighborhood
    Build Bridges Through Good Citizenship
    Acknowledge the Ultimate Bridge Builder
    Share Your Bridge Building Ideas with Others
  Political Correctness Madness 65
  We Need a Conversation 65
    The Dangers of Balkanization
    Past Injustices
    Progress
    Conversation With Solutions
  Healing That Heals 67
    Claims of an Activist
    Need for Efforts that Heal
    Need for Better Spokespersons
  Letter To The Editor: Response To The Response:
    Healing That Really Heals 70
    Commemorative Marches Are Beneficial
    Holocaust A Poor Analogy
    Need for Tempered Statements
  Letter To The Editor: Bipolarizing Native American History ... 72
  Letter From A Dakota, John La Batte To Frederick Wulff 73
  Conference: Multicultural History And The Native Americans ... 76
    Christian "Correctness"
    Political "Correctness"
    Historical "Correctness"
    Cultural "Correctness"

    Pre-history "Correctness"
    Seek Scholarly Authors
    Experience Native American Culture
    Use Native American Sources
    Use Biographies of Native American Leaders
    Use State and Federal Sources
    Use Classroom Activities
    Use Current Events
    Use Scripture

Chapter Three: Education 92
    Everyone Is A Winner! Or Are They?
        The Consequences Of Grade Inflation 92
        The Number of Valedictorians
        Grade Inflation Began in the Colleges
        Grade Inflation at the Middle and High School Level
        Grade Inflation at the Elementary School Level
        Real Competition for Grades Is Healthy
        Prepare Students for the Real World
        Integrity and Reporting Honestly
        Look in the Mirror
        The Remedy
    Response To Everyone Is A Winner… Grade Inflation 105
    Public School Teachers Need Senority Rights 105
        We Should Retain the Experienced Teachers
        Respect for Service
        Making Exceptions
        Attracting Future Teachers
    The Teacher As More Than A Facilitator 107
        The Facilitator of Substance
        The Facilitator and Neutrality
        The Facilitator and Curriculum Standards
        The Facilitator and Post Modernism
        The Facilitator and Judgmentalism

Insensitive Teachers 112
Response To Insensitive Teacher 113

Chapter Four: Religion And Christian Life................................. 115
    Initiating The New Kid 115
        Initiation, or Is It Hazing?
        The Old School of Thought
        Opportunities for the Bully
        Emotional Scars
        Fond Memories or Nightmares?
        Giving Offense
        Making Adjustments
        No Nonsense Guidelines
        Assimilating the New Kid with Christian Kindness
    Shameful Traditions 125
        "Lost" Traditions
        Administration Involvement in Traditions
        Eradicating Shameful Traditions
    Sociology With An "S" (Like In Sin) 127
        Individual Responsibility and Sin
        Institutions, Providence and Sin
        The Marriage Institution and Sin
        Dysfunctions and Sin
        Deviant Behavior and Sin
        Cultural Differences and Sin
        Peer Pressure and Sin
        Group Behavior and Sin
        Genes and Sin
        Environment and Sin
        Conscious Choices and Sin
        Absolution and Sin
    Sociology Presentation... 136
        Introduction
        The Limitations and Value of Sociology

    The Social-Conflict Paradigm
    The Structural-Functional Paradigm
    The Natural or Biological Paradigm
    Classroom Application of Sociology
    Spiritual Values
    Cultivating A Wider View
    Absolute Values
Civility 147
    Petty Nitpicking Politics
    Polarization
    Character Assassination
    Fight a Good Fight
"Christian Politics": The Best For Both Worlds 149
    A Fundamental Lesson from the Word
    Learning from History
    Politics as a Worthy Vocation
    Serving "Our" Constituency
    Solving the Problems of Society
    The Need for Debate and Exchange of Ideas
    Seek "Honest History" Free of a Political Agenda
    The Primary Role of the Church
Defining Marriage As Between A Woman And A Man 157
    Position of Conservative Christians
    Positions of Sociologists
    Position as a Civil Right
The Parallels Between Islam And Mormonism 159
    Known to Unknown
    Revelations/Holy Books
    Ongoing Revelations
    Historical Inaccuracies
    Rapid Growth
    Schisms
    Revered Shrines
    Prescribed Outward Behavior

    Views on Sin and Redemption
    Materialistic Hereafter
    Conclusion
  A Strange Journey To Becoming A Church Worker 167
    Family Background
    Becoming a WELS Member
    God's Miraculous Ways
    The Role of Faith
    God's Blessings Though the WELS

Chapter Five: Common Sense And Miscellanous 173
  Clean Up The Incognito Mess 173
  Travel To Tunisia 174
  Bureaucracy-Itis 176
    The Bad Image of Bureaucracies
    The Roots of Bureaucracies
    Bureaucracies as Good for the Church
    Pitfall #1 Inattention to Individual Cases
    Pitfall #2: Stifling of Initiatives
    Pitfall #3: Bureaucratic Growth
    Pitfall #4 Inclination to Control
    Perceptions Within the Church
    In Conclusion
  Enough Is Enough 184
  Boycotting For "Christmas" Is Economic Terrorism 184

INTRODUCTION

The title of this book may seem an oxymoron, but some people have a belief system of downright contradictions. These are people, as is the author, always evolving and never really fitting into a set pattern. Perhaps one could call that rugged individualism, but that term does not capture the intent suggested by the title. Rugged individualism was the phrase used often by Herbert Hoover during his time as president. It refers to the idea that each individual should be able to help themselves out, and that the government does not need to involve itself in people's economic lives nor in national economics in general. It is often associated with "social Darwinism" or an "up-by-the-bootstraps" philosophy. Well, in a way that describes the conservative nature of this author. A nanny government can foster an over reliance of government for everything and stifle individual initiative. However, at the same time the author's liberal nature maintains that the government can and should be helpful in promoting change and to provide a safety net for those in dire straits through no fault of their own (like natural disasters). This trait of "liberalism" takes issue with President Eisenhower's statement that the government cannot and should not "legislate morality." Ike's do-nothing philosophy seemed to justify indifference to glaring needs of dealing with social issues such as the evil of racial segregation. I believe he was misguided in this position. The secular government can and should pass laws that curb harmful actions against its citizens. Lutherans often refer to this as "civil righteousness" (but not imputed righteousness).

The word independent in the book title is intended to convey being free from blind conformity to a particular group. This independence doesn't mean being quirk-like just to be a non-conformist. When teaching college classes I did not wear bib overalls, braid my hair or use pot just to impress students or to rile society. To sum it all up, just think of this writer as a maverick instructor who would never quite fit into a predictable box-like mold in order to say what each situation merited.

The author's independence is reflected not only in the political sphere (having never voted a straight ticket during his long life), but extends to the fields of sociology, education and religion. He believes many sociologists have gone off the deep end, and have made unwarranted conclusions in spite of evidence to the contrary. Sociology can be a very useful subject, but not when it is used to force an agenda. In the area of education, teaching methods and curriculum content tend to be trendy, but common sense and reflections should never be outdated. In the area of religion, churches understandably develop strongly held traditions, but these traditions should not be carved in stone. As a Christian church worker the author contends only the Bible contains absolute truth, a reliable map that offers directions without glitches.

Using the expressions of Hayakawa in his book *Language in Thought and Action*, the "maps" in our minds are or should be constantly changing as experiences in life modify our outlook to more accurately reflect the territory (reality). My own lifetime of experiences, together with a strong Biblical outlook, continually corrected my perceptions, to help me better understand the real word, to see things more clearly. This has led me to be open and to write quite candidly. Some people like to play it safe and hold their cards close to their chest, but I prefer to be candid and lay my cards on the table. Positions expressed herein represent only those of the author and his updated "maps." Hopefully some of the readings will help readers modify their own "maps" to better fit the territory.

Some of the submissions that follow may seem to be dated, but I believe the substance still has relevance for the present.

CHAPTER ONE
HISTORY AND TEACHING HISTORY

MAKING SENSE OUT OF HISTORY: FOOD FOR THOUGHT

Originally published in The Lutheran Educator, volume 47, number 1, October, 2006

A Disturbing Trend: Disjointed History

As I was returning to the United States from a tour of Rome in January of 2007, I noticed a young lad on the plane across the aisle from me reading from a history textbook. I surmised that he was keeping up with assignments missed while visiting Rome with his parents. I tapped him on the shoulder to make an inquiry. As I suspected, he was an eighth grader from the States on leave of absence from school. When I expressed interest in his textbook, he kindly consented to loan it to me.

As a former principal with eighth grade teaching responsibilities, and later as a college American history professor, I had evaluated a number of history textbooks in my day. This textbook was different. It did not take long to come to the conclusion that what I was reading was nothing more than a compilation of politically correct topics which encouraged "critical thinking, " gave disparate groups equal time and spared the reader substantive historical content. To me this seemed like an apple pie without apples. Equally disturbing, I felt the book lacked cohesiveness -- no major theme or real focus on America's past. This led me to the contributing authors page at the forefront of the text. The main author was one with whom I had been familiar from national history conferences -- one that took pride on forging revised standards for teaching American history. I also noticed that instead of a list of historians in the various fields of American history, the coauthors represented special interest fields with an agenda to push. This was a nice mix for those who like a mix, but should not a text have more historical cohesion than what appears as a compendium of *Readers Digest* articles?

The Unraveling of History – The Loss of Cohesiveness

Throughout the ages, historians have tried to make sense of historical records by weaving the threads into some kind of comprehensible fabric. In a recent essay entitled, "Narrative, Periodization and the Study of History," Dr. Theodore Rabb of Princeton University makes an interesting observation: "When there is no magisterial, let alone coherent, story to tell, history loses its force as an engine of civic education." He astutely recognizes that the trend in the past thirty years or so has been for professional historians to intensely fragment scholarship and to narrow research to topics, which often neglect the broader picture and sense of narrative. Professor Rabb recognizes that these microhistorians with their disconnectiveness "can have serious effects on the other responsibilities that historians share to give a coherent account of their findings to a wider public." His major concern was the consequence for the young whom we teach. Furthermore he contends, "There can be no doubt that the fragmentation that has intensified during this period has been one of the reasons for the declining standards of instruction and the shrinking knowledge of history in most Western countries" (*Historically Speaking*, January/February, 2007, pp. 2-4).

One of my foremost areas of concern in the textbook cited was the lack of attention given to the Colonial and Revolutionary periods of United States history. I believe that unless our students are familiar with and understand the big picture -- the overall contributions of the Founding Fathers, the influence of former political traditions, the uniqueness of colonial experiences and the forging of our Constitution, they cannot appreciate our present form of government. The richness of our heritage can be lost if we dwell on isolated bits and pieces instead of the whole. There is a recognizable pattern in history that teachers should draw upon. This framework provides a meaningful reference point from which we can and should apply critical thinking skills.

The Fallacy: There Is Your Truth and There Is My Truth

There is danger in the mentality that promotes throwing up the hands and saying: "There is so much historical information out there that we can only pick and choose!" No wonder we are becoming, or rather have become, a nation of historical illiterates. When there is no basic story to tell, one is merely cherry picking. With this thinking, any account, regardless of substance, is considered as good as another. When ideologues and activists use the cinders of facts (or invent them) for their own purposes, students are vulnerable to their jihad mentality and conspiracy theories because they are ignorant of history. Off the wall demagogues simply say," There is your truth and there is my truth." Most of us are familiar with recent publicity surrounding the cause celebre from the University of Colorado, Boulder (Ward Churchill), the University of Wisconsin, Madison (Kevin Barrett) and University of Minnesota, Duluth (James Fetzer).

You may recall that Churchill taught that the victims of 9/11 were little Nazis. Barrett alleged that 9/11 destruction was staged by the United States, the war on terror is phony, the 2005 London bombing and the 2004 Madrid bombing were committed by U.S. or western military intelligence and not Islamic terrorists. Fetzer shares those views and also argues that Minnesota Senator Paul Wellstone's death in an airplane crash was not accidental but resulted from a conspiracy to ensure Republican control of the U.S. Senate. The net effect of disinformation, selective accounts and incoherence merely diminishes the influence of all scholarly historical work.

A Dilemma: Over-Compensation with "Cherry Picking"

Is history the story of man's depravity? Are there periods in our nation's history that we should lament? There is no doubt that history is a story of man's sin. So many of the problems throughout history (racism, greed, lust for power, aggression, political corruption, etc.) are the result of the Old Adam. Here we seem to be in agreement with the postmodernists who see only evil in our country. But as George Marsden, professor of history at the University Norte Dame, correctly points out: "Many historians today, driven by commendable interests in giving the oppressed or the neglected their due, distort the historical record by presenting it as though all the blame in a conflict is on one side." Marsden goes on to say that sometimes groups will try to balance the record by writing histories that only celebrate the disparaged groups' virtues and achievements to redress earlier misrepresentations and damaging images. (George Marsden, "Human Depravity: A Neglected Explanatory Category," *Figures in the Carpet*, published by Wm Eerdmans, December 2006). Cherry picking can bring about an extremely negative image of our nation. History teachers should avoid that pitfall by teaching within an overall broader context and Christian schoolteachers should keep in mind that history is also the story of God's grace, even though it may not always seem evident. Do not start with the shallow assumption the United States is an evil empire.

Examine the Whole Picture: Drink Deep or Taste Not

Where is a valid historical perspective if we do not bother with the whole picture? Do we gain understanding by looking at only a few withered trees rather than seeing the whole forest. Should the lobbying efforts of those with an ax to grind prevail over a rational study of a subject area? This does not mean we should dismiss harsh realities. Nor should we slight critical thinking skills. Looking back at the Colonial period, I believe that if George Washington and Thomas Jefferson are evaluated, even with "warts and all" in their roles as contributors to the young nation, they will come out better than just evil slaveholders. A study of the George Washington administration might include an evaluation of cabinet selections, court appointments, foreign policy, financial policy, law enforcement, integrity and dedication as the first president. His ownership of slaves should be viewed in historical context – truthfully and honestly, but not in isolation. Students need a broader understanding of history, one that may not be gained by superficial "critical thinking" from pick and choose tidbits.

We can sympathize with the fine excellent university systems that pride themselves on academic excellence and scholarship only to be embarrassed by a few shallow ideologue professors. It is encouraging to know that professors like Rabb of Princeton and Marsden of Norte Dame have come forth with a healthy remedy to combat this malady.

History is a fascinating subject and brings nourishment to the mind. Have a complete diet, fill the whole plate and thus avoid mental malnutrition.

SPEAKING OUT

TEACHING SOCIAL STUDIES WITHOUT A NEGATIVE PARADIGM

Originally published in *The Lutheran Educator*,
volume 45, number 2, December 2004

Is the United States a Terrible Country?

When we teach our social studies classes, do we sometimes find ourselves stressing the negatives so much that we leave the impression that we who live in the United States have little to be thankful for? Our present-day United States really is not such a terrible country. The government does not dictate content of textbooks. People are not dying in attempts to flee across our borders for haven elsewhere. It cannot be denied that we have shortcomings as a nation, for we live in a sinful world. But let's look at our history in perspective. In contrast to most countries, we have, in the course of little more than 200 years, developed many liberties, rights and freedoms. Actually, we have much more than we deserve -- surely where sin did abound grace did much more abound. With all the frailties of human institutions, we have been graciously blessed. We would be ungrateful if we did not acknowledge God's grace and the blessings of living in a free land, especially since the Gospel had and has free course. Constant dwelling on the negative in American history may shut out the attitude of thankfulness and praise that God rightfully deserves.

Is there a danger of glossing over the darker events in our American history? Stonewalling has happened in Japan, and more recently in Russia. A just published high school textbook in Russia, *History of Russia and the World* by Nikita Zagladin, is virtually mute on the deportation of ethnic groups under Stalin. The omission prevents students from a full understanding of their history (Maria Danilova, "In Russia, sometimes you can tell a book by its cover: High school text glosses over abuses," AP. *Star Tribune*, August 22, 2004, p. 17). We should not advocate any such blatant cover-ups in our teaching, but neither should we omit our better moments. One of the strongest criticisms leveled against our country is that our society is racist. No doubt racism has been part of our history -- that is sad and factual -- but is that the only thread in our national fabric? Some critics delight in pointing out that George Washington and Thomas Jefferson owned slaves; and there have even been instances where school districts have changed the names of schools from the names of the Founding Fathers to distance themselves from "those racists." But to be honest and to look at the Founding Fathers in historical context, they emerge as visionaries in an age when disgusting bondage and discrimination was an unfortunate and acceptable way of life. We might concentrate also on the courageous struggle for civil rights and the need for a positive blue print for future progress. Some noble individuals, like Martin Luther King, Jr., paid dearly for challenging bigotry and placing racism on the public agenda. Of those within the established government, John Quincy Adams deserves a bow, even though the negativists would deny him the honor. In the late 20th century, the nation itself really started to breathe the fresh air of human rights. In hindsight, it is easy to condemn even those like Harry Truman who were on the cutting edge of civil rights, simply because he used the prevailing language of his time. Keep in mind, Truman almost lost a presidential election in 1948 because his stand on civil rights alienated the Dixiecrats and some members of his own party. Let's encourage our students to continue the quest for equality and to use as models those who strove for justice and fairness in an age when it was not politically expedient.

Needed Stress on a Positive Multiculturalism

With an increasingly smaller world brought about by easier means of travel and widespread telecommunication, our contact with different races and cultures has shattered our parochialism. Immigration dynamics have brought a mix into our classrooms. We need to take a positive approach to those whom God has brought into our midst. The National

Council for Social Studies has issued a statement that sums up the need for integrating multiculturalism into curriculums: "To build a successful and inclusive nation-state, the hopes, dreams and experiences of the many groups within it must be reflected in the structure and institutions of society. This is the only way to create a nation state in which all citizens will feel included, loyal, and patriotic" (NCSS Task Force on Ethnic Studies Curriculum Guidelines, Curriculum Guidelines for Multicultural Education, A Position Statement of National Council for the Social Studies [Washington, D.C.: NCSS, 1976, revised 1991], p. 3).

Classroom instruction in social studies should reflect our Christian concern for a fair portrayal of contributions from other races and cultures. When we teach about the painful relocation of Japanese-Americans during World War II, let us also mention the role of the Nisei soldier in the 442nd regimental combat team and the 100th infantry battalion, which was the most decorated unit in all of W.W.II. Asian Americans are the fastest growing population in the Midwest and it is important, for that reason, to include more information about them. We could also add that nationwide, Hispanics make up an increasing portion of the population and have contributed much to our culture. Inclusion of these Americans is very necessary. Most of the states, in which the WELS operate Christian Day Schools, have population centers of Native Americans and the Synod has long had an outreach with Apache Indians in Arizona. We surely should give Native Americans emphasis in our own social studies standards. The struggle of minorities to adjust and to find a place in the larger society is woven with stories of people who had courage and vision.

The Perversion of Multiculturalism

Unfortunately, there has been a trend among some well meaning but misguided educators, historians and political activists who have turned the noble endeavor of multiculturalism into a travesty that really has only hurt the cause of minorities. Syndicated columnist Thomas

HISTORY AND TEACHING HISTORY

Sowell, an African American, laments this tendency. He believes that one of the reasons our children do not measure up academically to children in other countries is that "too much time is spent in American classrooms twisting our history for ideological purposes... Propaganda has replaced education as the goal of too many educators." Too often these kinds of teachers "look at the past with the assumptions -- and the ignorance -- of the present." The best way to counter this kind of teaching is through a better understanding of historical perspective (Thomas Sowell, "Twisted history," New Ulm *Journal*, December 19, 2003). Post modernist thought has demoted the quest for truth and objective scholarship and has substituted in its stead a shallow acceptance of politically correct propaganda.

Some students in college history classes are taught we are an evil nation with a history dominated by villains. Here in Minnesota, Professor Mato Numpa of Southwest State, Marshall, wants children of kindergarten age taught that Columbus deliberately practiced genocide on Native Americans and that contagious diseases were only part of his devious plan. Furthermore this same professor compares the government of Abraham Lincoln with that of the Nazis and leaves no room for debate. He states unequivocally that Lincoln's military in Minnesota gave inspiration to Hitler for his policies of the Holocaust. Those who disagree with him in this assessment are brushed off as either "racists" or "in denial" (Staff writer, "Southwest State University professor says Hitler patterned torture after U.S. genocide techniques," New Ulm *Journal*, November 9, 2002). Surely, Native Americans were grossly mistreated in Minnesota and in the nation as a whole, thus fabrication is unnecessary. The historical records are clear and the truth speaks for itself. The Native American cause does not need reinvented history because truthful history is on their side. Many current leaders concentrate on hate mongering to garner support for their leadership positions rather than working for the betterment of their ethnic or racial base. (Frederick Wulff, "Bipolarizing American History," editorial, New Ulm *Journal*, November 13, 2002). The ranting of militants, with their politically correct distortions, should not deter us from the legitimate need for multiculturalism.

Critical Thinking or a Negative Agenda?

Should we encourage critical thinking in our social studies classes? Definitely! We need our students to be well informed and to evaluate differing viewpoints in order to become discerning citizens. History and studies in current events help students to see through shallow and stilted reasoning, even when it comes from "scholarly" college professors. Again, here in our region, a Minnesota State university, Mankato professor made a public statement in New Ulm that the only free press left in the world is Al-Jazeera. Are students led to believe that the presses in authoritarian Muslim Arab countries are free to express dissent while the American press hides the truth? Rather, this shallow comment about the Arab press reflects a commonality with those who hate our country and believe we are "evil". The assumption is that if our country would turn from its evil foreign policy, terrorists would not have targeted us. A little investigation would show that Muslim fundamentalists target many areas outside American influence where they simply strive to impose a Muslim dominated society. Consider Indonesia, the Philippines, Chechnya (Russia), Algeria, Chad, Nigeria, etc. We have to guard ourselves against those who believe that if an account is hateful about our country, then it must be good reporting.

Those of us familiar with Professor David Noble of the University of Minnesota, Twin Cities, have witnessed negativism personified. In one American history class when a disgusted student asked Dr. Noble if there was any hope for the future of our nation, he responded, "No. Because, even if minorities gained control of the country they would just become part of the establishment." The examples of professors previously given are all from the state of Minnesota, but the state is not unique in this respect. The nationwide Organization of American Historians, of which I was a member for twenty-five years and faithfully attended their annual conferences, used to be the number one professional organization for history professors in the country. Recent dominance by political activists had led to shouting matches and a stifling of scholarly debate. This ultimately led many members to resign and form a splinter organization.

We should resist a "critical thinking" which seems to be just a criticism of anything done by our country. Those who use this criticism paradigm exclusively often start with stereotypes of "Euroamericans," a racist term intended to be derogatory. From this premise they place themselves in the pitfall of forcing history into a preconceived pattern. Where is the critical thinking in the classroom if uninformed students merely parrot predetermined negative responses? Imagine taking a course from a teacher or professor who is locked into this negative framework mentality, and see how much critical thinking is allowed those students who do not accept his/her pronouncements. If the instructor has no use for objectivity, how many students would sacrifice their course grade, or standing in the class, to offer a different viewpoint or to point out contrary evidence?

Responsible Instruction

Of course, there are many respectable and responsible professors and teachers who do attempt to provide a positive atmosphere of objectivity and foster a climate that encourages free debate without intimidation. Most minorities do not agree with radical self-appointed or self-serving leaders who are of a rigid mindset mentality. Katherine Kersten, board member of the Center of the American Experiment, says, "Most Americans view the United States as a noble experiment which, despite its flaws, is eminently worthy of their love and loyalty. In a 1998 Public Agenda poll, 84 percent of parents agreed that the United States is 'a unique country that stands for something special in the world.' Eighty-three percent of parents overall and 81 percent of African-American parents reported that they would be 'upset or somewhat concerned' if their children were 'taught that America is a fundamentally racist country'" (Katherine Kersten, "Critics would teach about an oppressive America," *Minneapolis Star Tribune*, November 9, 2003).

Love and understanding brings true healing. The Gospel can and does provide us motivation to treat others as we would be treated. All races and minorities are of one blood and the blood of the Savior has redeemed all. Mistreatment of others, throughout history, should provide lessons so that injustices are not repeated. History can give us hope and a personal understanding that the actions of all people, even the ungodly, will ultimately serve His purpose. This makes the past meaningful.

Current Events – History in the Making

We can take a positive spin on current events by encouraging objectivity in the discussion of daily news reports. Instead of seeing political parties and their candidates in an oversimplified context as good versus evil, we can foster the notion that there are honest differences of opinion on how the citizenry may best be served by elected officials. There really are candidates of both parties that are honorable. We should encourage students to avoid demonizing the opposition. This is a real challenge for teachers because we live in an age when crude nastiness often prevails during election years. Many say that this bitterness and invective thrive because the press contributes to this mentality with its disrespectful coverage of our presidents -- both Democratic and Republican. If elections tend to center on defamation of character rather than an important difference on issues, we might want to encourage letter writing that threatens withholding support from candidates whose campaigns engage in character assassination. Try to have your students concentrate on real issues. Help them to see the differences of the political parties and their formulas for dealing with the economy and social concerns. Promote the gathering of as many facts as possible to clarify issues. Then have open discussions on why people develop strong differences on those issues. Historical perspective can also give tremendous insights into the understanding of current problems.

In Conclusion

Because of sin, we do not live in a perfect world. Government officials and their policies are often flawed despite good intentions. One of the ways God blesses us is through government that provides a semblance of order in a world of disorder. It is that stability that allows us to preach the Gospel and to maintain our Christian institutions free from chaos and harassment. Pray for our elected officials and stress the importance of well-informed voters. Avoid the negative paradigm that fosters hopelessness and stifles voting participation. Strive for civility and fairness in our classes with a respect for historical truth, warts and all -- while being mindful that we should not be an ungrateful and thankless people.

WEAKNESS IN SOCIAL STUDIES TEXTBOOKS

Originally published in The Lutheran Educator, volume 34, number 4, May 1994

Second Class is Not Good Enough

I believe that the most important quality of a social studies textbook is that it reflects good historical scholarship— that it is a reliable tool. A recent issue of *The Lutheran Educator* had a book review of a textbook by John Garraty that earned high grades in that respect (Wulff 1993). Historian Paul Gagnon, the principal investigator of the Bradley Commission, once wisely wrote: "History is, above all, a good story and the truth is always the best story to tell ourselves" (Gagnon 1989, 147). Conversely, the worst textbooks, in my opinion, are those textbooks that care little about accurate reporting— those that carelessly perpetuate myths and misconceptions in spite of solid contrary evidence. Some may argue that grade school texts should avoid complex cause-and effect situations or controversial interpretations because these students can only handle shallow and superficial treatment of a subject or just bare names and dates. That is a fallacious and demeaning argument. Grade school texts can and should have substance with an upfront and truthful approach. Charlotte Crabtree has well said, "Historical thinking, including causal analysis, takes many years to acquire, but its foundation is rightly laid in the elementary school" (1989, 182). There is no justification for poor textbooks that lack scholarly quality. There should not be a conflict between the material found in the grade school texts and that which children may see in a well-documented TV special or that which they will encounter in high school or college. Grade school students can handle truthful substance now. We are not here talking about "political correctness." Professor Diane Ravitch, a member of the Bradley Commission, says that those of all political persuasion should be interested in "seeing history taught honestly, as history" (1989, 89). I think all of us would like to put to rest those ubiquitous half-truths that seem never to die. It is essential that our textbooks are not misleading or need correcting—whether we use textbooks for daily assignments, developing units, assigning background reading, or just for reference.

Weaknesses that Perpetuate Myths and Misconceptions in Specific Areas

Let us first examine just what erroneous information has intruded into our national past and continues to live on in grade school textbooks. Many may be familiar with Thomas A. Bailey's *Probing America's Past: A Critical Examination of Major Myths and Misconceptions*. Although the book is not the last word, it does have merit for drawing attention to the many myths that still plague us. Of course, some differences

Bailey cites may be subjective opinions, but others are much more than that, and may justly be referred to as errors or outdated interpretations. A good starting point for noting weaknesses is the allegation of Paul Gagnon. Besides serving on the Bradley Commission on History in Schools, Professor Gagnon serves as consultant to the National Center for History in the Schools based at the University of California, Los Angeles. He expresses his concerns about textbook shortcomings rather convincingly in his book (1989). For example, Gagnon chides current textbooks that fail to clarify the early Puritan faith and aspirations in colonial America. For example, Gagnon believes many texts leave a false impression: "By failing to clarify [Puritan] faith and aspirations, the texts leave the impression that they were hypocrites— or more hypocrites than we are—for wanting 'freedom' for themselves but banishing those who question their theology and church authority," nor do the texts explain "why they believed they had compelling reason to abhor unorthodox religious doctrine" (Gagnon 1989, 37). Furthermore, according to Gagnon, "Modern readers, always ready to mistake their own indifference to religion for the virtue of toleration, could profit from a better perspective" (1989, 38). Thomas Bailey also discusses this and other misconceptions about the Puritan colonists. Bailey reminds us how Puritan religious leaders "tried hard to exclude from the tender new spiritual vineyard unorthodox foxes that might ruin the grapes." He then goes on to say, "By the standards that existed elsewhere in most of America, and indeed in Europe, colonial Massachusetts enjoyed a refreshing amount of political democracy." As for Puritan attitudes toward science: "To their credit, a number of the New England clergy were among the foremost champions of science" (Bailey 1973, 1: 27-30).

The American Revolution, too, is fertile ground for myths. Theodore Hartwig opened the 1990 New Ulm Social Studies Symposium with an address in which he touched on this problem: "When writing history and telling its story, it must be the truth; and the nearer the story touches us, the more difficult this is. The story of our American

War for Independence as told in elementary school texts for many years suffered from much over-sanitation" (Hartwig 1990, 5). It is so easy to foster misconceptions under the guise of patriotism. How convenient it is to blame a "tyrant king" than to look at ideological questions that had risen between the colonies and the parliament of their mother country. Thomas Bailey directs much attention to the many stubborn myths surrounding the American Revolution and the events leading to the confrontation. For example, you may want to check if your textbook still carries the old Beardian notion that there was not widespread suffrage in the colonies. In this respect Gagnon, as well as most historians, notes that most males owned land and fulfilled that voting requirement. Gagnon goes on to say that suffrage "was still more widespread than elsewhere in the world, and popular elected legislators represented roughly equal numbers of people" (1987, 46). Charles Beard also left the impression that the oncoming Revolution was a class war. Gagnon warns against this notion, "Ours was a revolution largely free of class hatred. We had not suffered the privileged clergy and aristocracy of the Old Regime, or the manifest injustice of its legal system and taxes. Gaps between rich and poor were less extreme, class relations were less strained" (1989, 49). Some textbooks on American history still do not adequately address the failings of the Frederick Jackson Turner interpretation of the American frontier. Alan Brinkley of Columbia University in a recent review for The *New York Times* notes that central to new Western history is at least "an obligatory, almost ritualistic repudiation" of the Turner thesis for its ethnocentrism and celebration of democratic individualism (Quoted in Sewall 1993, 1). Unfortunately, few texts below the college level concern themselves with the validity of either the Beardian or Turner thesis. The list of outdated interpretations could go on and on. The Reconstruction period of history has been revamped since the 1950s, yet many of the old racist interpretations still linger. Twentieth century history, with all of its controversy, also needs to reflect the real issues people faced.

Weaknesses of Simple Errors

When it comes to finding errors in textbooks, the well-known names of Mel and Norma Gabler of Texas come to mind. The Gablers were kind enough to respond to my letter with a request for their material on social studies textbooks. I learned that Norma Gabler had presented a Texas State Board of Education Committee a list of 512 errors she said were contained in ten history books used in junior high and senior high schools. Most of these errors primarily involved dates. Others included cities, wrong events, and inaccurate numbers (Gabler 1992a). A State Board of Education textbook committee acknowledged that nearly 300 errors remain in U.S. history textbooks shipped in the fall of 1992 to Texas schools. Carolyn Crawford, who heads the school board committee, said publishers will be required to pay $300 per error, or nearly $90,000 in fines, as well as to provide correction sheets for the books. After looking over some of the errors listed by the Gablers, I believe the publishers would have caught most of them if historians had been employed as consultants. For example, the statement in one text, "House votes to impeach Nixon," should have been, "The House Judiciary Committee voted to recommend articles of impeachment to the full House." An incorrect capital of Vietnam should also have been caught, as well as a reference to the "Battle" of Valley Forge. Some of the errors caught by the Gablers, however, were a matter of personal interpretation and would stand up to the scrutiny of historians. For example, the Gablers question the prevalence of nationalism during the period of the Articles of Confederation. Recent studies support that "error." Yet, when it comes to searching out factual errors, the Gablers deserve credit in that respect.

The Weaknesses of Forced "Christian" History

It is not appropriate to twist or distort history in order to construct a "Christian" history. We need to respect the truth. We should seek the truth. Our students expect that from us. Naturally, as Christians we have a Christian perspective of history — that God controls history and that the destiny of nations are in his hands. This we accept by faith. However, outside the revealed knowledge of biblical history, we continue to search for historical knowledge much as do secular historians. During our lifetime we will not know everything about history or the meaning of every single event. If we claim to know what God means in all of our history lessons, students may equate our "Christian" history content and interpretations with God's absolute truth. We must remember that history books are always subject to change in the light of new research and scholarly studies, so we must always make it perfectly clear to our students the difference between God's absolute truth and the tentative history found in our textbooks.

The Gablers, no doubt, are sincere and well meaning in their efforts to promote "Christian" history, but there are serious flaws in their materials. In a twelve-page duplicated tract on the American Revolution distributed by the Gablers the author intends to "show how traditional rights of Englishmen were allegedly derived from Biblical absolutes" (Frey 1981,1). Bible passages are then used to support the contention that the British later acted against God's laws by having standing armies, quartering troops, and restricting freedom of trade. Under the explanation for what the author suggests was the "un-Christian" Proclamation Line of 1763 is the statement, "The enactment of the Proclamation had little to do with Indian affairs and nothing to do with Chief Pontiac's rebellion" (Frey 1981, 5). Historians of the frontier would find that statement outrageous. The tract then assaults the Quebec Act of 1774 as restoring "the old French feudal system so detrimental to the peasant farmers there" (Frey 1981, 10). Actually the Quebec Act was a wise and fair piece of legislation, fulfilling a promise to defeated people of French descent that the British would respect their rights to practice Catholicism and to retain French traditions in regards to land tenure. The only purpose of this tract's lengthy tirade against the British seems to be to show them as a godless people. Thus when this tract uses Bible passages to "prove" the need to remove the lawless rulers, the implication is that the rule of the 18th century British Parliament was godless. Those in the colonies who opposed the Loyalists, on the other hand, are assumed to be the agents of God. The Gablers attempt to justify the American Revolution because the British government was collecting unpopular taxes and they suggest, therefore, that colonials were doing God's will by rebelling against England. One could better argue that overthrowing a government is in conflict with God's Word (Ro 13:12). The material used by the Gablers also describes what they believe to be will of God for civil government. The Bible thus becomes a blueprint for civil government. The weaknesses in this kind of an approach have been discussed by Joel Gerlach, (1982). Pastor Gerlach wrote of those "who want to employ a tool (the Bible) that God gave his church to be a guide for Christian living as a tool of civil government" (1982,233). Reformed theology tends to force everything into a "Christian" framework to support a preferred civil policy and then to impose that policy at the expense of the church's real gospel mission. For example, in a tract on biblical principles on economics, the author cites Bible passages that he claims oppose graduated taxes on wealth and which support free trade, (Frey 1990a). The Gablers use their tract "Biblical Principles in the United States Constitution" (1983) to promote the use of Christian textbooks. This tract illustrates well the Reformed approach to claiming absolute knowledge of what God intended in each historical situation. When new scholarship necessitates revamping history and civics books, persons who take this approach will find themselves saddled with outdated interpretations which they have tied to God's will. For example, the tract seemed especially forced when it refers to Article VI of the Constitution as analogous to Scripture in the moral realm and to hard money in the economic realm" (Gabler 1983, 1) and of the separation of powers as a "direct analogy to the Trinitarian sharing of sovereignty in the Godhead" (Gabler 1983, 2). In another pamphlet distributed by the Gablers this Trinitarian concept is explained further: "Complete individuality (three Persons) coexists with complete unity (God) in the Trinity. Politically, the many particular individual states share sovereignty with the collective federal government—neither the individuals nor the one group being sovereign over the other and both following Biblical political and economic principles" (Frey, 1990b, 2).

One of the objections the Gablers have to secular textbooks has to do with "functional humanism." It isn't clear what is meant, but they include a belief in global citizenship as evidence of functional humanism. In their criticism of the United Nations, which they interpret as an ungodly organization, the Gablers warn us of this statement they found in a textbook: "Many people think a stronger U.N. or a new international organization is needed if we and other peoples of the world are to move safely into the 21st century. Only a stronger world body, they argue, can meet tomorrow's challenges." Immediately following this quote is this highlighted statement: "THESE VIOLATE A BIBLICAL PRINCIPLE: 'So the Lord scattered them abroad from thence upon the face of all the earth...' Genesis 11:8a" (Gabler 1992b, 5). This condemnation does not leave much room for Christians who might think international cooperation for peace through a world body is desirable. At least, this is a legitimate topic for discussion and it stretches the point to object to using a text that examines the role of the United Nations as a peacekeeping body. Certainly this is preferable to a locked mind-set that shuts off thinking under the guise of protecting Christian principles.

The Weaknesses of Omission and Fragmentation

Then there is the danger that some major areas are not treated at all—either by the text or the classroom teacher. The danger is cited in "Education for Democracy: A Statement of Principles," which was written in 1987 as a guiding charter for an Education for Democracy project. Some 170 prominent persons from Jimmy Carter to Ann Landers were signatories to the statement of principles. Among the concerns was the following: "The kind of critical thinking we wish to encourage must rest upon a solid base of factual knowledge. In this regard, we reject educational theory that considers any kind of curricular content to be as good as any other, claiming that all students need to know is 'how to learn'…that in an age of rapid change, all knowledge necessarily becomes 'obsolete'" ("Education …", in Gagnon 1989, 166). The content we teach is important and we should avoid textbooks that are bland and shallow in content or simply problem oriented. If we have developed a good curriculum that treats important areas of our historical heritage, then it would be well if we utilized the best resources to that end. If we are tolerant of textbooks that skip over major units for the sake of student interest, we are part of the problem in the social studies crisis. There are also textbooks, which present material in fragments in a misguided attempt to be "inclusive." Thomas Bender asks the question: "Is the primary task of historical writing to confer legitimacy on every group through representation, or is it to achieve interpretive understanding of the whole society and its past?" (Bender 1989, 189-190). With the legitimate concerns of multiculturalism, we need to give treatment to the varied contributors to the story of history. Professor Bender states that we can relate the different ethnic groups to the whole "by integrating them and not ignoring them or obscuring them" (1989, 189-190). This is not an easy task because of the various rights groups competing for center stage in the narrative. Gary Nash suggests that this integration can still be done without neglecting the traditional figures and institutions in history by showing the interaction of the great political and religious leaders, scientists, captains of industry, and military officers with the mass of ordinary people and to show how each group influenced each other (Nash 1989). But in this integration Paul Gagnon reminds us that "It is senseless for historians, whose first lesson is that time limits all possibility, to be fighting for space in a single year so fragmented by demands for multicultural education that our students fail to comprehend the roots and needs of the democratic political vision that best promises to nourish peace and justice in a multicultural society. The focus is on the West in this respect, is not because it is inherently better than other civilizations but because it has produced liberal democracy and many of the moral values that sustain it" (Gagnon 1987, 38-39).

Epilogue

If we use textbooks that require constant clarification about misleading content, the students will be confused. Then, too, poor texts require re-teaching later on. Re-teaching can be much more difficult than teaching. Teachers should avoid textbooks that do not use professional historians as consultants. In selecting textbooks, faculties need to compare the prospective textbook content with that of a quality college text written by a team of respected historians. This will also provide a refresher exercise in U.S. history. A collaborated college text by Paul Boyer, Clifford Clark Jr., Joseph Kett, Thomas Purvis, Harvard Sitkoff, and Nancy Woloch may serve well as a benchmark for this examination. (Boyer 1990). I suggest to my history students that they keep their college history textbooks as reference books. Professor Neil Stout offers the same advice: "There is a great temptation to convert textbooks into cash, but are you sure that you'll never have any more questions about American history? You can look things up in the library, but having your text at hand will save time" (Stout 1994, 79). Good advice for teachers who keep abreast of history and expect their textbooks to do the same. Good teaching methods are important, but just as important is the content of what you teach.

WORKS CITED

Bailey, Thomas. 1973. *Probing America's Past: A Critical Examination of Major Myths and Misconceptions.* 2 vols. Lexington, MA: Heath.

Bender, Thomas. 1989. "Public Culture: Inclusion and Synthesis in American History."

In Historical Literacy: The Case for History in American Education, edited by Paul Gagnon. New York: Macmillan.

Boyer, Paul, C. Clark, Jr., J. Kett, T. Purvis, H. Sitkoff, N. Woloch. 1990. *The Enduring Vision: A History of the American People.* Lexington, MA: Heath.

Crabtree, Charlotte. 1989. "Returning History to the Elementary School."

"Education for Democracy: A Statement of Principles." 1987.

In Democracy's Half Told Story: What American History Textbooks Should Add, by Paul Gagnon. Washington, D.C.: American Federation of Teachers.

Frey, Neil. 1981. "Biblical Principles: Rights of Englishmen and Acts of Parliament, 1763- 1775." Mimeographed.

Frey, Neil. 1990a. "Biblical Principles of Economics." Mimeographed.

Frey, Neil. 1990b. "Biblical Political Principles." Mimeographed.

Gabler, Mel. 1983. "Biblical Principles in the United States Constitution." Mimeographed.

Gabler, Mel. 1992a. "Textbook Fiasco Continues." Newsletter (December): 1.

Gabler, Mel. 1992b. "Humanism/Moral Relativism." Longview, TX: The Mel Gablers.

Gagnon, Paul. 1987. *Democracy's Untold Story: What World History Textbooks Neglect*. Washington, D.C.: The American Federation of Teachers.

Gagnon, Paul. 1987. *Democracy's Half- Told Story: What American History Textbooks Should Add*. Washington, D.C.: The American Federation of Teachers.

Gerlach, Joel, 1982. "'Christian' Public Policy." *Northwestern Lutheran* 69:232-233.

Nash, Gary. 1989. "History for a Democratic Society."

In Historical Literacy: The Case for History in American Education, edited by Paul Gagnon. New York: Macmillan.

Ravitch, Diane. 1989. "The Revival of History: A Response." *The Social Studies* (May/June): 8.

Sewall, Gilbert. 1993. "The American West." *Social Studies Review*

(Spring): 1-3.

Stout, Neil. 1994. *The History Student's Vade Mecum*, 2nd Edition. Lexington, MA: Heath.

Wulff, Frederick. 1993. "A Good Social Studies Textbook." *The Lutheran Educator* (September): 27-32.

A GOOD SOCIAL STUDIES TEXTBOOK

Originally published in *The Lutheran Educator*,
volume 34, number 1, October 1993

A special review

Frederick H. Wulff

Text *The Story of America* by John Garraty (Holt, Rinehart and Winston, 1991)

Grade level: seventh and eighth grades

Scope: the first Americans to the present (1219 pages), divided into 10 units and 30 chapters

Ancillary Materials:

The Story of America Audio Program (11 tapes for student review); Annotated Teacher's Edition Voices of America: Speeches and Documents (1 tape); The Story of America Workbook (126 pages); The Story of America Assessment Book with tests and evaluation; Creative Strategies for Teaching American History (360 pages); The Constitution: Past, Present, and Future (114 pages); American History Map Transparencies (22) with thematic overlays and teacher's discussion guide; Art in American History Transparencies (49 transparencies); Art in American History Teacher's Discussion Guide with Worksheet (126 pages); Time line posters (2) illustrating important events in history.

The Bradley Commission Recommendations

When the Social Studies Department of Dr. Martin Luther College hosted a symposium "Equipping the Saints for Citizenship through the Social Studies," we considered the concern for more substantive teaching of the social studies as advocated by the Bradley Commission. We also addressed ourselves to the various ways the objectives of social studies might be better achieved. After the New Ulm symposium, members of the division took mini-symposiums on the road to the various districts in the Synod. At one of these mini-symposiums in Wisconsin I was asked the question: "If we are to upgrade our teaching of social studies as advocated by the Bradley Commission, what would be good textbooks that would help us to meet those high standards?" As I began my answer to that question, I started with the assumption that the Bradley Commission was on track when they expressed dismay "that many school districts now allow optional classes, some called 'area studies' and with little history content, to substitute for the 8th grade course" (Commission 1988,3). I personally feel the eighth grade curriculum should meet stiff criteria. I also believe that to attain these criteria the selected text should lead to learning that reaches beyond the acquisition of useful facts to nurturing such habits of thought as are essential to the discipline of history.

State Recommendations

To start off my quest for a "substantial text," I turned to the state of California. California has been in the forefront of the process to improve the social studies curriculum and encourage textbook reform. The Table of Commissioners who oversee the state curriculum and textbook adoption process accepted the recommendation of a state review panel which recommended the Houghton Mifflin series for the lower and middle grades and Holt Rinehart's *The Story of America* for grades seven and eight. Sixteen other books, submitted by seven different publishers were rejected (Sewall 1990). Other state commissions have come to the same conclusion. Among the six books adopted by Texas in 1991 was *The Story of America*. The South Carolina adoption was the most selective. Fourteen books were submitted to the state, including most of the major U.S. histories developed and introduced in the last two years. Among those adopted was *The Story of America* (American Textbook Council 1992). What most distinguished *The Story of America* is its author, John Garraty. John Garraty of Columbia University has a national reputation as a historian and more than five million college students have used his college text. WELS teachers who have attended DMLC recently used his *The American Nation* (Seventh Edition) for the American Scene course. He also knows how to put together a text for the eighth grade. When the Organization of American Historians met in Reno, Nevada, in 1990, John Garraty was asked to present a major address on what makes a good history textbook. John Garraty is an Advisory Board member of the American Textbook Council, "a national consortium to advance the quality of textbooks and all instructional materials." He is also a member of the Organization of American Historians, which has endorsed the efforts of the Bradley Commission.

Scholarship

Since a primary consideration for choosing a social studies textbook is scholarship, authorship and the use of historians as consultants are very important. What we teach is more important than how we teach. John Garraty himself made use of 20 specialists who read portions of *The Story of America* in manuscript. Among the American history professors acknowledged are John Morton Blum, Arthur Link, Edmund Morgan and Robert Remini.

The Textbook Author as Educator

The *Story of America* is not only scholarly, it is highly readable. Garraty's narrative is filled with anecdotes that will catch the students' interest. Throughout the book students are often asked to use their historical imagination and to place themselves in the roles of others. I believe that the liberal use of primary source quotes that bring students authentic voices from the past is a noteworthy strength that stirs the historical imagination. Garraty not only helps students understand America's past, he helps students develop basic study skills, critical thinking skills, and social participation skills. To this end he has 32 "Strategies for Success," each placed at a point in the text where it may be most appropriately applied. Strategies include map reading, reading a time line, and interpretation. Many of these strategies involve cooperative learning and student involvement. The textbook is attractive with many beautiful and functional illustrations in color. Maps are uncluttered. Charts, tables, diagrams, and graphs have been designed for simplicity and clear presentation of new information. The Annotated Teachers Edition has wide margins that surround a slightly reduced student text. Conveniently located here are many worthwhile suggestions, including teaching resources, strategies for students with special needs, multimedia materials, chapter objectives, motivational activities, closure options, suggested homework assignments, and much more.

Treatment of Constitutional History

The Bradley Commission states, "Most obviously, an historical grasp of our common political vision is essential to liberty, equality, and justice in our multicultural society" (Commission1988, 6). *The Story of America* meets that standard. Garraty gives appropriate attention to our western heritage and the development of the Constitution. He notes the connection of the contract theory of government, the separation of powers, and other political developments as having roots primarily in western Europe. According to Professors Paul Clineand Anthony Eksterowicz (James Madison University), one of the most important topics covered in both American history and government textbooks is the struggle for and debate over the ratification of the Constitution. A major criticism of leading textbooks is that they devote very little attention to Antifederalist arguments and positions. These two professors wondered how historians would approach coverage of this debate in their textbooks. To answer the question, they examined 17 American history textbooks on the college, high school, and middle school level. The books studied included John Garraty's *The Story of America*. Others used in the comparative study were James Davidson and John Batchelor, *The American Nation* (Prentice Hall, 1990), Robert Divine, et al. *American: The People and the Dream* (Scott Foresman, 1991), William Jacobs et al. *America's Story* (Houghton Mifflin, 1990), and Clarence Ver Steeg, *American Spirit* (Prentice Hall, 1990). The methodology of the study included looking at both manifest and latent content in the comparisons. Manifest content was determined by the number of citations included in sub-headings, captions, pictures, and cartoons. Latent content involved coding the quality of textbook treatment of Antifederalist arguments. In areas of comparison by paragraphs, pages, and balance, John Garraty's *The Story of America* outranked all of the others. The authors believe that "the failure to present in-depth coverage of both sides of the ratification debate is important because this debate largely defines our nation" (Cline and Eksterowicz 1992, 70-71). John Garraty's book had nine paragraphs with Antifederalist treatment and 12 paragraphs of Federalist treatment. I believe this study brought out strength in Garraty's work.

Relating Geography to History

The Bradley Commission states that students should "understand the relationship between geography and history as a matrix of time and place, and as context for events" (Commission 1988, 9). John Garraty draws upon the wisdom of Phillip Bacon, Professor Emeritus of Geography and Anthropology, University of Houston, as his geography consultant. Garraty can boast that in his text the vital influence of geography on the growth of the United States is a dominant theme. Every unit includes a two-page essay called "Linking History and Geography." These essays integrate the themes of location, place, and relationships within places, movement, and regions. There are more than 80 maps that are clear and colorful. Each map includes learning from the map section. The set of transparencies has excellent maps, especially those that show the physical features of America.

Relating Religion to History

The Bradley Commission sees as a "vital theme" for study "the several religious traditions that have contributed to the American heritage and to contemporary American society" (Commission 1988, 12). There can be do doubt that Christianity has played a major part in our nation's story. I believe Garraty has not overlooked this in his text. Among American professional historians there is a striving for historical truth, a desire to make the narrative more faithful to the past we share. Recently historians have been encouraged to tell the "whole truth" with respect to the role of women and minorities. Yet, publishers and teachers of history have often been timid in attention to the sensitive area of religion— often no action at all has been the easier course. When religion is excluded from American history the factual content is lost, says historian Edwin Gaustad: "With respect to chronicle of the past, religion is a datum and point of reference as omnipresent and inescapable as the rivers and the mountains, the laws and the courts, the trade routes and the labor unions, the political parties and the national presidents" (Gaustad 1992, 17). I believe Garraty shows balance and fairness in his treatment of religion in our history in *The Story of America*.

The Treatment of Women and Minorities

The Bradley Commission resolved "That history can best be understood when the roles of all constituent parts of society are included; therefore the history of women, racial and ethnic minorities, and men and women of all classes and conditions should be integrated into historical instruction" (Commission 1988, 8). The *Story of America* transparencies on works of art and worksheets on artists both incorporate the contributions of women and minorities. Besides good integration of material about minorities into the narrative of the text itself, there are special portfolios depicting the ethnic diversity of American society. The American Indian, West African, Hispanic, and Pacific heritages are all represented, each with four page illustrated essays. Women's history and literature is woven into the narrative of the unit or lesson. Prominent women are also featured. As do virtually all textbooks, this one follows the guidelines for non-sexist language.

Creative Strategies

The auxiliary materials are quite impressive. Teachers will find the manual "Creative Strategies for Teaching American History" very valuable. Obviously one may not use all 80 teaching strategies, but a teacher can incorporate wisely from the wide range of topics and activities. Most of the strategies involve cooperative learning in which students work toward a common goal. In his introduction Garraty does note that teachers should stress personal responsibility and individual accountability when making assignments. Usually each worksheet, which may be duplicated for class use, provides historical background, a list of materials required, and suggested procedure. I was especially impressed with the liberal use of primary sources. Another supplement is the manual "Art in American History" with a teacher's discussion guide and worksheets. This manual is to be used in conjunction with a set of beautiful transparencies depicting representative art works throughout our history. The quality of the transparencies is very good, capturing the colors well. The selections include not only the better-known artists like Homer and Remington, but also works of women and artists from various cultural backgrounds. Each worksheet gives essential background information on the artist and the work of art. An "Interdisciplinary Connections" section enables the teacher and students to place a piece of art in a historical context between art and social or historical development. These art lessons would work well integrated into the regular social studies class periods, since art reflects the physical, social, political, and cultural changes of a nation.

HISTORY AND TEACHING HISTORY

The Time Element and Grade Placement

If a Lutheran elementary school were to adopt this textbook with its rich resources and varied teaching/learning strategies, would the teacher need to allot a great deal of class time to the teaching of history? Yes! Social studies must have a prominent part in our daily schedule. The National Council for History Education, carrying the message from the Bradley Commission and the National Commission on the Social Studies, is pressing for all teachers to be given the chance to teach quality history classes. In the chronological narrative of our country, the Council states there must be "frequent pauses for studies in depth," time to deal with "significant, compelling themes," and opportunities to "demonstrate the interdependence of history and the humanities." Garraty's text should be used over the course of seventh and eighth grade rather than just eighth, so we don't find ourselves "madly rushing from the Ice Age to the spring prom" (Gagnon 1991, 43).

Despite all the good features of this text, I do not advocate that the WELS school have an official textbook for eighth grade. *The Story of America* has much to offer but each school should go through a curriculum review and textbook selection process. The American Textbook Council has announced it will release in late 1993 a standard of review for social studies textbooks. This guide to quality will review issues of content, style, and design. It will also include ratings of the major textbooks in history, geography, and civics. The guide will be distributed free of charge to subscribers of Social Studies Review1 and it will be available for sale. You may also wish to consult the *Data Book of Social Studies Materials and Resources*, edited by Leslie Hendrickson.

2 I also recommend *Current Directions in Social Studies*.3 Both will help you in the task of textbook selection. But without question, *The Story of America* merits a most careful consideration in your selection process.

NOTES

1 American Textbook Council, 475 Riverside Drive, Room 518, New York, New York 10115.

2 Social Science Education Consortium, Inc., 855 Broadway, Boulder, Colorado 80302.

3 C. Frederick Risinger. *Current Directions in Social Studies*. Houghton-Mifflin, 1992.

WORKS CITED

American Textbook Council. "Reading Tea Leaves." *Social Studies Review* 11 (Spring 1992): 11.

Bradley Commission on History in Schools. Building A History Curriculum: Guidelines for Teaching History in Schools. Washington D.C.:

Educational Excellence Network, 1988.

Cline, Paul and Anthony Eksterowicz. "Textbooks and the Ratification of the Constitution: A Review Essay," *Magazine of History* 6 (Spring 1992): 67-72.

Gagnon, Paul. "National Council on History Education," *Magazine of History* 6 (Summer 1991): 42-43.

Gaustad, Edwin S. "American History, With and Without Religion: ... 'the whole truth... so help me God,'" *Magazine of History* 6 (Winter 1992): 15-18.

Sewall, Gilbert T. "California: The Story Continues," *Social Studies Review* 6 (Fall 1990), 10-12.

MOVIES AS HISTORY

Originally published in *The Lutheran Educator*,
volume 38, number 4, May 1998

Movies on Television

No doubt students enjoy watching history as if it were taking place before them with all the scenery and sound effects. Some studies indicate that students do not read as much in this television age; rather, they rely more on visual signs. Filmmaker Ken Burns says that visual images "will become the glue that makes memories." Our students are being exposed to many documentaries and special series regularly on television. Some of these are quite well done. Possibly we can even tune students in to these scheduled programs beforehand. In 1990 Ken Burn's The Civil War, an eleven-hour series, broke the PBS audience record for an education series. An estimated 13.9 million Americans watched the first program with many more, estimated at 40 million, tuned into the later programs. Since then millions more saw subsequent broadcasts or watched them in classrooms. We definitely do not want to downplay reading, but teachers can take advantage of the video offerings.

Develop Historical Empathy

The Bradley Commission on History in the Schools has noted "History instruction must help students perceive past events and issues as they were experienced by people at the time, to develop historical empathy as opposed to present-mindedness." This prescription might be partially accomplished with carefully selected movies. We need powerful story telling as a framework for history with a natural sequence; many movies and documentaries do flow in narrative fashion. At the same time a number of movies may lend themselves to meaningful discussion sessions. Why not use the better movies to flesh out the bones from the past? To their credit the motion picture industry has become very adept at bringing people and events to life. With special effects and recent technology they can capture almost any imagery. Although some movies may be excessively offensive because of gratuitous sex and violence and not adaptable for our use, there are some good movies, documentaries, and special series suitable for the upper grades and secondary schools.

Seek Historical Accuracy

Movies must be more than entertaining or exciting, important as these qualities may be. The primary concern of any social studies teacher should be to seek the most truthful accounts of historical events possible, and consequently to have students seek out historical accuracy when they watch movies. Is it possible to find out the truth about the past? This should be our quest. As Christians we have a high regard for honesty and finding the truth. Unfortunately, a prevailing Oliver Stone mentality complicates our task and the public is sometimes subjected to extravagant claims based on the slenderest of reeds. Dr. Lynne Cheney, in a recent interview, lamented, "apparently the Oliver Stone version of reality has replaced historical reality." Certain movie directors like Stone feel that not having all the answers surrounding an event or events is a justification for deception and untruth, but they only muddy the historical waters. If moviemakers wish to indulge in purposeful distortions for the sake of artistic creativity or lively fiction, that is their prerogative. But they should not palm off fiction as history. Historian Eric Foner commented in a book, *Past Imperfect*, "God knows how many people now think Jim Garrison (in JFK) had the assassination all figured out." I believe that the movie, The Lincoln Conspiracy, based on a book by Balsiger and Selliers could serve as another object lesson in how profit-seeking individuals can muddy the waters of history. The Hollywood authors make the claim that they have unearthed "shocking new evidence" to prove their conspiracy theory. If this were an honestly held viewpoint, history might be well served, but the movie is a purposeful distortion based on untruth.

Be Informed

How then can we judge an author's honesty and commitment to providing truthful knowledge on a particular subject? First, we need to learn the subject area ourselves. Teachers should be lifelong students of history. They cannot be satisfied with superficial knowledge that excuses shallowness with "there is just too much history." Second, we need to look for the names of reliable consultants used in the production. Third, we can search out reviews by professional historians who have established reputations in a particular area of history. In the case of The Lincoln Conspiracy, we might consult a review by David Lindsay of California State University which points out that the story depends upon Edward Baker, a man who had a grudge against Secretary of War Stanton and was known by contemporaries as a notorious fabricator and whose words were not supported by reliable sources.

Distorted History: Movies with an Agenda

Both students and teachers should realize the importance of background research and critical thinking. Critical thinking should cultivate awareness that movies may distort historical accuracy by a present-mindedness— to take events from the past and twist them to suit current mind-sets. We might ask whether the artists were willing to tell history as it should have been or like it really had been. Ken Burns maintains he did the best possible job with The Civil War in evoking what it must have been like at the time. He had his critics from "the new historians," but his response was, "Only those who seek to use history for polemical ends can find real fault in this approach." Films also offer teachers an opportunity, says professor Harvey Jackson, "to get students not only to evaluate the accuracy of what is depicted, but to ponder why the film was made as it was." Lynne Cheney believes that sometimes accounts are presented "not to get at the truth, but to create a picture of the past that is socially useful." Edmon Martin, a major researcher on early slavery including the now-famous Amistad incident, was happy the movie Amistad spurred attention to the slave rebellion, but complains it misrepresents the faith and the role of 19th century abolitionists. The movie plays down their contributions and trivializes their profound religious faith. He was quoted as saying, "I can see why that would be congenial to contemporary American culture, but it really misrepresents American history." Teachers need to watch for present-mindedness that forces history to tell a story to justify a current ideology. History may serve to be socially useful and to broaden our cultural outlook, but history should not be rewritten or invented retaliation just to mold student opinions.

A Word to the Wise

Can we be too critical of movies that attempt to put life into dry dates and facts of seemingly little meaning? Is it possible that historians can be such nitpickers that they stifle creativity and artistic projects? Ken Burns once blamed "the Germanic academic model from the end of 19th century that really spelled the end of popular history." He went on to say that other historians "helped kill the public's appetite for history." Good history has always been a balance between capturing the truth of events and breathing life into the drama of events. We should ask for both. Burns, in a conversation with David Thelen, acknowledged he had come to "depend on historians for their expertise to guide me through many projects." A reasonable solution is to have creators of a historical epic (if it claims to be history) enlist the use of historians as consultants. There have been attempts by a number of filmmakers recently to authenticate their work by using prominent historians as consultants. One notable example is The Blue and the Grey (an eight hour mini-series on CBS), which made use of the distinguished Civil War authority Bruce Catton. Ken Burns himself in his The Civil War asked historians C. Van Woodward (who enlisted James McPherson), Shelby Foote, and David McCullough to serve among the 22 consultants. The Civil War: A House Divided was another a well-done video that used the talents of John Hope Franklin as an adviser. Professor

HISTORY AND TEACHING HISTORY

Jenkins suggested that networks employ historical consultants, just as medical or legal consultants have been employed in recent years. Those who produce and direct documentaries for TV could greatly benefit from historians; historians in turn should appreciate the artistry of television producers.

There are also movies that are not really history, but take place in a historical setting. Such movies are really not documentaries but they may serve as discussion points about the period portrayed. James Fenimore Cooper's novel, *The Last of the Mohican* was recently the subject of a movie. Historian Richard White in his review of the movie ripped into it with obvious relish, but director Michael Mann defended his work: "I wanted history to become as vivid and real and immediate as if it were being lived right now." Of course the movie was based on the novel, but we could note the strengths and weaknesses of its depiction of historical events. Teachers may want to have students look up the historical account of Fort William Henry, the importance of the British support in the French and Indian War, or the role of the frontiersmen during the conflict. Then, too, teachers could compare the review of White with other reviews.

There are teachers that make use of historical novels as a way to study the past with good results. As noted above, an excellent way to check on the merits of historical truthfulness in a movie is to look up movie reviews by professional historians. In a recent book, *Past Imperfect: History According to the Movies* sixty of the world's most lauded historical writers look beneath the celluloid surface of popular movies to examine the relationship between film and the historical record. According to the book's jacket, "Best selling authors as Gore Vidal, James McPherson, Antonia Fraser, William Manchester skewer, praise, pick apart, and otherwise illuminate these cinematic portrayals of history, telling us as much about what the filmmakers got right as about where they went wrong." The book is edited by Mark C. Carnes, chairman of the history department at Barnard College, Columbia

University. Put out by the Society of American Historians, the book covers a spectrum of films from Spartacus and Julius Caesar to Anne of a Thousand Days and both films on Christopher Columbus up to Mississippi Burning and JFK. Some movies have value in a historical sense. Prominent Civil War historian James McPherson reviewed the popular movie Glory.

McPherson starts with a question: "Can movies teach history? For Glory, the answer is yes." He goes on to say that it is also "one of the most powerful and historically accurate movies ever made about the Civil War."

Sources for Movie Reviews

An excellent hard cover book of reviews is *Past Imperfect: History According to the Movies*; sit may be found in most libraries.

Most larger libraries have issues of the *Journal of American History*. Robert Brent Toplin, editor of the Movie Reviews in the journal, has had numerous movie reviews over the years. Reviews in this Organization of American Historians publication began to turn up in numbers starting with the December 1996 issue ("History on Television: A Growing Industry," Vol. 83, numbers 3-4). Among the 27 recent titles reviewed in that edition are Patton, George Wallace, and Andersonville. The recent December 1997 edition has numerous professional review offerings, which include Thomas Jefferson produced by Ken Burns (1996), Hawaii's Last Queen (1997), Ghosts of Mississippi (1997), and The People vs Larry Flynt, produced by Oliver Stone (1996).

Besides the movie reviews found in the widely circulated news magazines such as *Time* and *Newsweek*, reviews may also be found in *American Historical Review*, *History and Theory* and *American History*.

HISTORY AND TEACHING HISTORY

Sources of movies for social studies

- Instruction Filimic Archives. Toll free 1-800-366-1920 or custom service number 203-268-1796. Ask for their Videocassette catalog.
- The American Experience PBS videos. Call toll free 1-800-344-3337. They have a 62 page catalog with content summaries of their videos offered in 1998.
- Direct Cinema Limited, a company that advertises its films and videos in the Magazine of History. Call toll free 1-800-525-0000
- Learning Corporation of America, customer service department 1-212-397-9360
- Teacher's Video Company: American History 1998 has a comprehensive 95-page catalog of every aspect of our nation's history. They also have a 79 page catalog World History & Social Studies 1998 for just about any country. In either catalog the videos are listed as $29 each, with a buy 4, get 1 free offer. 1-800-262-8837.
- The A&E Network has launched the History Channel—HTV which features history related movies, miniseries, documentaries, and dramas. A monthly TV calendar of HTV history offerings is available on the Internet (http://www.historychannel.com/)

SELECTED BIBLIOGRAPHY

Building a History Curriculum (Bradley Foundation, 1988)

Mark Carnes. *Past Imperfect: History according to the Movies*, John Holt Co., Society of American Historians, 1995).

Lynne Cheney. *Telling the Truth: Why Our Culture and Our Country*

Have Stopped Making Sense–and What We Can Do About It (Simon Schuster, 1995).

Edmon Martin quoted by Maja Beckstrom. "Moving Beyond the Movie," St. Paul *Pioneer Press Express*, D1, February 14, 1998

Harvey Jackson, "Can Movies Teach History," *OAH Newsletter* November 1990.

William Jenkins. "Why TV Needs Historical Consultants," *OAH Newsletter*, November 1990.

Lawrence Linderman. "Indictment," Modern Maturity, January-February 1998.

David Lindsay. Review of Lincoln Conspiracy, *Journal of American History*, December 1978 (Organization of American Historians).

David Thelen. "The Movie Maker as Historian: Conversations with Ken Burns," *Journal of American History*, December 1994 (Organization of American Historians).

Robert Brent Toplin. "History on Television: A Growing Industry," The *Journal Of American History*, December 1996 (Organization of American Historians).

Robert Brent Toplin. *Ken Burn's The Civil War: Historians Respond* (Oxford Press, 1996).

TEACHING SOCIAL STUDIES: THE CONTROVERSY OVER STANDARDS

Originally published in *The Lutheran Educator*, volume 45, number 1, October 2004

Introduction: The Neglected Subject

A strong case can be made that teachers and administrators have shuffled instruction in social studies to the bottom of the deck. Those of us who have taught college courses in American history have noticed a discernible change among entering students over the years. Students seem to know less about their nation's history with each passing year. It is not just a question of faulting either public schools or private schools, for this trend appears quite universal.

If high school graduates across the nation are as weak in the knowledge of U.S. history as polls suggest, think of the future of the nation if prospective teachers attend a college where American history is not even taught or is diluted in some world studies course. There are university history professors who lament the fact that college students can avoid American history courses entirely and still graduate from their program in education.

In the past, the Profile of Learning guided Minnesota public schools. In a study commissioned by the Thomas B. Fordham Institute, Sheldon Stern complained that Minnesota's Profile of Learning standards for social studies, "in keeping with the substantively watered-down approach advocated by many American schools of education since the early 20th century, reject anything resembling a real academic curriculum." One critic complained in the *St. Paul Pioneer Press*: "We don't need students bogged down in pointless Profile projects, like carving sculptures for a European history class, classifying movies and dogs for a high school science class or using board games and pop movies to do research for a high school history course -- to cite just a few examples I've seen." In 2000, the Council for Basic Education judged the Profile to be "inadequate preparation" for a solid sequence of history and civics courses in high school."

This slighting of social studies is not only in Minnesota. Michigan is another case in point. Lori Higgins, an education writer for the *Detroit Free Press*, laments that three-quarters of Michigan's teens in the Class of 2003 couldn't meet the standards in the subject. Since the social studies portion of the test debuted in 1999, Michigan never has had more than 26.6 percent of high school students meet or exceed the standards. Social studies experts' worry one of the reasons is that the emphasis on the three R's is turning social studies into a neglected subject. If social studies are devalued the consequences for our nation are severe. The national No Child Left Behind (NCLB) law has had the effect of marginalizing social studies education at all levels, but especially at the elementary level. Since federal mandates under NCLB do not include civics or history, they are being dropped in many schools to allow more time for testing in the mandated areas. The Fordham Foundation argues that if NCLB is not modified it will have done more to eliminate history and/or social studies than any other event, person or movement. If we do stress the noble subject of reading more, we do well to include substantive reading assignments on social studies topics.

The Minnesota Standards: Lightning Rod for Controversy

A heated controversy has been brewing in Minnesota over what should replace the discarded Profile of Learning, which had been criticized as too heavily weighted in favor of process. A committee of 44 teachers, parents and business representatives appointed by the state Department of Education commissioner, Cheri Pierson Yecke, recently wrote a proposed set of social studies standards. Yecke herself is a former history teacher. Chester Finn Jr., president of the Thomas B. Fordham Institute, notes that Commissioner Yecke came to Minnesota from Virginia, where she helped write history standards for that state that are widely judged among the best and most rigorous in the nation. She faced criticism there, he adds, but overcame it. Finn concludes: "Virginia's children are benefiting from her vision and her perseverance. We hope that Minnesota youngsters will be able to do likewise." The first Minnesota draft drew some criticism. After considering massive input from the public, Commissioner Yecke presented a final revised draft to the 2004 Legislature

Hard work and effort went into creating the new standards, and they have been improved with substantial modifications. The debate that the standards has provoked is beneficial reading. It behooves the faculties of our Lutheran schools to follow such debates (http:// education.state.mn.us and www.mcss.org) and set our own appropriate standards for quality instruction. Social studies, after all, is a critical subject that provides us Christians the opportunity to both promote knowledge and appreciation of our country as well as critical thinking necessary for responsible citizenship.

The Argument for Stress on Historical Content

Some comments submitted to the Minnesota Department of Education applauded the first draft of standards because it weighed heavily on content. Julie Quist, director of EdWatch/Maple River Coalition, a vocal group that fought for the repeal of the Profile standards, maintains a knowledge-based system is important. "Knowledge is not useless," Quist argued. "It is very valuable for the building blocks of being able to do critical thinking. You can't bring students into a classroom and teach them critical thinking until you have a body of knowledge that they can think about." Another supporter of Supervisor Yecke, stressing emphasis on content, is Gary Marvin Davison who praised the revised standards: "A sequenced, content-rich, highly specified liberal arts education made available to all children in our diverse society is the most powerful engine of social and economic equity."

The final body of knowledge advocated in the revised standards, to its credit, is more than a list of facts. Quite a few critics of the initial standards expressed the view that content a mile wide and an inch deep made no sense. The Minnesota Association of School Administrators commended Yecke for pressing for rigorous standards, but recommended that the focus should be on identifying major concepts to be taught at each school level as opposed to detailed listings of fact. A massive number of facts and dates may obscure the important larger focus area. Obviously, information acquired through interesting narrative or well-planned units is retained longer than just items on a list. Specific items must be learned in a comprehensive context. And as for dates, they have value only if they are made meaningful within a time line framework and are necessary to visualize sequence.

The Need for Critical Thinking in the Standards

Some would argue that critical thinking is "process" and that it does not belong in the standards. Actually, it does belong, along with content. To understand history and the lessons that can be learned from it, critical thinking is extremely important. Good citizenship requires that we use critical thinking, which helps us as citizens to correct wrongs in the government and to support that which is noble. Children must learn that the nation, warts and all, was shaped by dissent, rebellion and debate, not simply blind allegiance. Critical thinking and analysis do not necessarily demonstrate hatred or disloyalty. Dissent can be healthy. A lively opposition in government within a two party system offers differing viewpoints and a balance. Sometimes a third party contributes a needed dose of fresh ideas. And then there are the contributions of many courageous women and nonwhites who struggled with the system for a place in society. The Minnesota Association of Secondary School Principals concluded: "Only by admitting, exploring, and analyzing these faults of American history alongside America's triumphs… will we be enabled to learn from our shared past and resolve its complicated legacies." They chide the initial proposed Minnesota standards for discouraging such analytical thinking. The National Council for Social Studies rightfully encourages presenting multiple perspectives when teaching history or any of the social sciences such as economics and political science, where a variety of interpretations and viewpoints exist: "Teach students that understanding causality, searching for evidence, and respecting the tentative nature of a considerable part of knowledge are valued habits of mind and heart."

Standards that Promote Democratic Institutions

A number of professors from the University of Minnesota rejected the Minnesota standards' benchmarks for government and citizenship, along with its history benchmarks. They objected, for example, to a first-grade standard that "encourages good citizen traits like honesty, courage, patriotism and individual responsibility." Why this opposition? They submit that portraying such traits as important components of citizenship is tantamount to "teaching patriotism as a reflex action of blind obedience or conformity." One critic of the standards wrote "patriotic symbols, songs, and events represents the worst type of nationalistic propaganda and must be eliminated from the standards." However, many prominent educators and politicians agree with this particular aspect of the standards. Recently, the Albert Shanker Institute of the American Federation of Teachers issued a consensus document called Education for Democracy. "As citizens of a democratic republic," the document proclaimed, "we are part of the noblest effort in history." Our nation's schools, it went on, must encourage "a deep loyalty to American political institutions and prepare students to protect and extend this precious inheritance." The document's signers spanned the ideological spectrum, and included former President Bill Clinton, Sen. Edward Kennedy and Reg Weaver, president of the National Education Association.

The Ongoing Controversy and Politics

The public is clamoring for reform, demanding higher standards and more accountability from schools. The teachers' unions resist change and fight all notions of accountability. They use their political muscle to influence legislatures and selection of state education officials. Here in Minnesota they successfully blocked confirmation of Commissioner Yecke, who had been on the job for more than 14 months. The Senate Education Committee, which is dominated by DFLers firmly in the pocket of the teachers union, voted along party lines to advise the full Senate to fire Education Commissioner Yecke. The standards had been revised before she was dismissed, and then later revised again in a closed-door session by a conference committee. Reform will not come easy. Yecke was criticized for being too controversial, but any attempts at reform will be bitterly contested by those who favor the status quo.

Standards that Serve Students

May this debate help us to avoid an "either or" mentality as we set up or review our own standards in our schools and help us to strike a healthy balance between facts and analysis that best serves our students. Above all, let's hope a discussion of this nature aids us to put social studies instruction on a front burner where it belongs.

Anyone familiar with our MLC students and Synod teachers knows they are highly motivated, hard working and dedicated individuals. One could argue that it takes courage to avoid the pitfall of contemporary society that has been softened by lower expectations and less accountability from students. Those of us who have interviewed foreign exchange students in our country are familiar with their testimonies that schools in their respective countries are much more demanding. Grade inflation and a comfort zone that rewards mediocrity do not really improve self-esteem, nor does it prepare students for the real/hard world. At the risk of sounding too conservative, we might be a little more traditional (actually, reform minded) than the mainstream by maintaining higher standards in social studies, and strengthening those areas being neglected or overlooked.

HISTORY AND TEACHING HISTORY

CREDIT WHERE CREDIT IS DUE: TALENT IN OUR MIDST

Letter to the Editor published in the New Ulm Journal, *May 15, 2012*

The Lifesytle section of the New Ulm *Journal* really brings different aspects of our community to life and helps us appreciate the talent in our midst. This last weeks Sunday edition (May 13, 2012) was true to this concept. I appreciate that the *Journal* brought attention to original research on the Sioux Uprising that had been accomplished by local people. Research on this topic was sorely needed to help fill in the missing pieces of the event. John Isch and Darla Gebhard are to be commended for doing such extensive and original searching which must have been unbelievably challenging. It appears the authors left no stones unturned to produce *Eight Days in August*. Previously so little was known about the settlers who were killed during the conflict, or even the number of those who perished.

The Dakota Trials by John Isch should help us to follow the "other side of the coin" by tracing the Dakota who had been pardoned by Abraham Lincoln, as well as the future of their families. Both authors should be commended for their professionalism and for leaving judgments up to the readers. No doubt there are many of us who look forward to reading these books when they are published.

Another gifted researcher in our midst is John LaBatte who deserves coverage as well. He has extensive knowledge about the Dakotas who resisted warfare and those like Red Iron who spoke out in defense of settlers who had been held captive. He also can shed much light on the Dakota who were taken to Fort Snelling afterwards. Since he had relatives among the Dakota on both sides of the Conflict, he has insights worth sharing.

Those who have an interest in an update on the US-Dakota War of 1862 need look no further than New Ulm.

SPEAKING OUT

REMEMBERING JOHN DICKINSON

Frederick Wulff

Originally printed in *DMLC Messenger* 1987

Countering an Unfavorable Image

As we celebrate two hundred years under the Constitution we are mindful of some rather remarkable Founding Fathers. Some are well known for their towering roles in writing and implementing the Constitution. But there is one among those men who gathered in the Philadelphia of 1787 that we often overlook, the honorable John Dickinson from Delaware. Today some only remember him as he was portrayed in the play (and movie) "1776" - as a delegate from Pennsylvania upstaged by the great John Adams. Yes, he was the gentleman who could not bring himself to sign the Declaration of Independence. However, that was but one scene in the life of John Dickinson. He paid dearly for his convictions and his principles in 1776 when he remained loyal to his king, when he held on to the hope that relations with England could be restored and improved. Because of that unpopular decision Pennsylvania did not reelect him as a delegate in 1777. And we still slight him in our classrooms, even though he was to become one of our major Founding Fathers.

Penman of the Revolution

John Dickinson spent his life in public service, and his contributions to our nation began long before he participated as a moving force in the Constitutional debates in Philadelphia. Although we have labeled him "a conservative," he was no foot-dragging conservative. He shunned what he called "the benumbing stillness of overweening sloth." Nor would he be tolerant of those who trample on the rights of others "however remote it may seem from our vitals." He had earned himself the distinctive title "Penman of the Revolution" for his championing the cause of colonial rights in the 1760s. He inspired the organized inter-colonial opposition to short sighted parliamentary measures. He was the main author of the "Declaration of Rights and Grievances" adopted by the Stamp Act Congress in 1765. Although a leader in the opposition to the Stamp Act, he also opposed all violent resistance, as well as the non-use of stamps by lawyers.

Christian Respect for Government

In 1767 Dickinson began publishing his influential "Letters from a Farmer in Pennsylvania" stressing the broad legal principles underlying English liberty. He could not ignore English infringements on traditional liberties: "When the liberties of one's country are threatened, it is difficult to be silent." He spoke out with conviction when he declared the Townshend duties unconstitutional. Yet he also understood that sound government is necessary for the survival of civilization, and something that should be respected even in difficult times. He made that clear when he wrote in one of his famous Letters: "Let us behave like dutiful children, who have received unmerited blows from a beloved parent. Let us complain to our parent; but let our complaints speak the language of affliction and veneration." Having been raised as a devout Quaker, Dickinson hoped that tension could be resolved with words. He warned the colonists not to be swayed by agitators who commit rash acts in the name of patriotism. Orderly resistance, however, did not prevail. Some Americans were more prone to violence. John Dickinson, who had great love for his king, pride in time-honored British traditions, and fondness of the Empire, could only lament:

> Where shall we find another Britain? Torn from the body to which we are united by religion, liberty, laws, affections, relation, language and commerce, we must bleed at every vein.

SPEAKING OUT

Citing the Rights of Englishmen

In the First Continental Congress Dickinson showed a clear grasp of the legal and practical tasks. At that time most colonials agreed on the nature and legitimacy of the petitioning process. It was his respect for peace and orderly negotiations that caused him to lead the middle colonies at the Second Continental Congress to press for moderation. It was Dickinson who composed the Olive Branch Petition adopted by the Continental Congress in July of 1775, which begged the king to prevent further armed conflict until reconciliation was arranged. Significantly this placed the blame for conflict on "those artful and cruel enemies who abuse your royal confidence and authority for the purpose of effecting our destruction," rather than on the king. Yet his conciliatory efforts failed. After skirmishes at Lexington and Concord, Dickinson wrote most of the "Declaration on the Causes and Necessity of Taking Up Arms" that was subsequently adopted by the Congress. In this he was determined to insist on the rights of Englishmen for the colonials. He noted colonials would "die freemen rather than like slaves." Still he cautioned: "We mean not to dissolve that union" between the colonies and English. But by May, John Adams and the Congress were moving in the direction of outright independence. When Richard Henry Lee presented resolutions for independence, John Dickinson spoke as expected in opposition and at great length. And when it came down to the actual signing of the Declaration, he simply refused to sign the document with his colleagues. Realities soon dictated cooperation with colonials -- the breach could not be spanned. As the American Revolution took its course Dickinson did join the militia as a private to demonstrate this cooperation and rose to the rank of general. While he was serving on the battlefield the British sacked his house in Philadelphia.

Formulator of the Articles of Confederation

The Articles of Confederation, which we often refer to as the steppingstone to the Constitution, was mainly the work of John Dickinson. On June 20, 1776, shortly before independence was declared, Congress appointed a committee, chaired by John Dickinson, to draw up a plan of perpetual union. *The Dictionary of American Conservatism* (New York, 1987) states "his major cause was states rights," but the facts demonstrate he favored a strong central government even while he was constructing the Articles of Confederation. Already in July of 1776 Dickinson prepared a draft national constitution. He knew the colonies needed a strong government with central authority, but he was too far ahead of his time. The report his committee presented on July 12th shocked delegates who assumed that the constitution would authorize a loose confederation of states. The Dickinson draft outlined a government of considerable power. Each state was to retain "the sole and exclusive regulation and government of its internal police," but only "in matters that shall not interfere with the Articles of Confederation." His plan to put all the western territories under congressional control fueled tension between states over land claims. His work was sent back to committee and reworked until eventually there emerged a "league of friendship." The draft Congress approved in 1777 bore little resemblance to Dickinson's original plan. The new constitution sent to the states for ratification was greeted with a mixture of apathy and hostility. This governmental arrangement was finally adopted by all the states in 1781, when Maryland insisted that western lands be ceded to the Congress. The central government under the Articles had no way of enforcing its authority. For six years the American cause depended on the inadequately empowered and uncertain Continental Congress.

Dickinson presided as chairman at the Annapolis Convention in 1786, which formally requested that Congress and the several states call a full-fledged constitutional convention to meet in Philadelphia. He and his fellow "conspirators" James Madison and Alexander Hamilton (the leader of the group) asked that the Articles of Confederation be "revised". When a convention was held in Philadelphia Dickinson tried to limit the scope of the convention to revision because he thought the Congress legally authorized only revision.

John Dickinson should be remembered as a man who disrupted his life at the age of fifty-five to lead the Delaware delegation at the convention -- not for personal ambition or hope of gain but by a recognition that the time had come for a "national deliberation." He had considerable experience in the art of government. For five years he had served the colonial government under the Articles of Confederation. Dickinson had acted as president of Delaware 1781-1782 and as president of Pennsylvania 1782-1785. At the Convention he displayed flashes of genius that is born of experience and political realism. Already on June 2, John Dickinson arose to speak and wisely pointed out that the delegates could save themselves a good deal of time and trouble by making the legislature bicameral, with representation apportioned in one branch and with each state having one vote in the other. But few were yet ready for compromise at that point. Later, after much debate, he saw that same concept carried out in what became known as the Great Compromise.

Contributions to the United States Constitution

Our Constitution embodies much of the best of English traditions. The Constitution helped to make time honored liberties secure through stable government. For this John Dickinson deserves much credit. He always remembered the wealth of his English political heritage and at the Convention he often made reference to that heritage. James Madison recorded him saying on August 13, 1787: "Experience must be our only guide. Reason may mislead us. It was not Reason that discovered the singular & admirable mechanism of the English Constitution. It was not reason that discovered or ever could have discovered ... the absorb mode of trial by jury ... And has not experience verified the utility of restraining money bills to the immediate representatives of the people?"

Supporting Ratification of the Constitution

When the convention reassembled for the last time in September, the sick, exhausted Dickinson had to leave for home a day early. In his absence a friend signed his name to the document. After the Convention many of the framers served in the new government they had created. Dickinson felt the strains and pains of public life and did not run for office again until his health improved. However, in 1788 he did write a series of articles under the name "Fabius" advocating the ratification of the Constitution in Delaware and Pennsylvania. His work was rewarded. He had the satisfaction of seeing his own state of Delaware become the first state to ratify the Constitution, and thus become the first state of the new nation.

The last years of Dickinson were spent in Wilmington, Delaware, where he joined the Friends' Meeting House. He reverted to the language of the ""thees and thous" that he had once used as a child. When he died at the age of seventy-five he was buried in the Quaker graveyard in Wilmington under a modest marker that is less than a foot high. His gravestone suggests he has been overlooked. His lifetime of public service suggests it should be otherwise.

POLITICAL ACTIVISM IN THE ORGANIZATION OF AMERICAN HISTORY

Letter of resignation: Frederick Wulff to the OAH in 1998

I have been an active member of the OAH for almost 30 years and have enjoyed attending the annual conferences. Because of recent events in the organization I am resigning in protest. The upcoming OAH conference was to be held at the Adams Mark in St. Louis, but militant activists employing economic terrorism have targeted this fine hotel. I find it irresponsible for the OAH to yield to a few militants and cancel hotel reservations on such short notice. This hot dog action will cause tremendous economic losses to a fine hotel that has set aside large conference halls and many rooms for us. The charge of racism on the part of Adams Mark in St. Louis is hollow. They employ mostly blacks, many which sorely need those jobs. We had a conference there in the past (which I attended) and the service was outstanding, so much so that the OAH Planning Committee scheduled them again for the upcoming conference. The charge that another Adams Mark hotel located in Florida upset a black man about baggage handling is an isolated incident and surely does not justify breaking a contract with a business in St. Louis.

I will switch my membership, as others have done, to The History Society, which conducts it organization in a professional and responsible way. I prefer membership in an organization not so influenced by political extremist that are interested in only promoting his or her own agenda.

Frederick Wulff

New Ulm, Minnesota

Added note: I received no response to my letter.

CHAPTER TWO
RACE AND MULTICULTURALISM

BUILD BRIDGES TO OTHER CULTURES

Originally published in The Lutheran Educator, volume 44, number 3, February, 2004

The Opportunities for Building Bridges

In today's society we have more chances than ever to interact with others from different cultures. Our Lutheran schools and congregations have taken on a multicultural look that would have amazed our forefathers. God has brought more diversity into our communities and schools so that we can build bridges. Teachers are in a great position for this assignment and their influence will have a positive impact on the make up of our future WELS membership. The classroom is an excellent construction site for this important project. No doubt many of our Lutheran schools are already at the task, but current situations provide even more opportunities to give attention to this vital project. Incorporate this mission into your classroom devotions, religion instruction and social studies units. Teachers can be effective architects for this worthwhile undertaking of building bridges.

Prepare for Bridge Building with the Word of God

To bridge cultural differences with others, the essential starting point for Christians is the Word of God. The construction material of the Word gives us a lasting and sure foundation. Our erosive sinful Adam has the tendency to look down upon those who have different skin color or those who have customs different from our own. The power of the Holy Spirit helps us overcome our human nature. All of us need to pray for hearts free from prejudice.

In the eyes of our Redeemer there are no hyphenated categories. St. Paul tells us, "Do not cause anyone to stumble, whether Jews, Greeks or the church of God -- even as I try to please everybody in every way. For I am not seeking my own good but the good of many, so that they may be saved" (I Corinthians 10:32-33). God would have us treat others, as we would have others treat us. Our love and concern for all people must have a priority in our lives. Good discipleship requires our best efforts to build bridges that span perceived differences. We should heed His words, "As far as it depends on you, live at peace with everyone." (Romans 12:18). Fortified with God's Word, we will have the heart, the strength and proper motivation for this undertaking of bridge building.

Develop Bridge Building Skills by Studying History

Our effort to understand and to appreciate people of other cultures is greatly enhanced by delving into history. A study of history will shed light on the diversity of cultures and social institutions among the world's races and nationalities. This background helps us understand the outlook and attitudes of others. To illustrate, while doing dissertation research on the Shawnee Native Americans, I developed a deep, lasting respect for them as a people. Reading original documents from the archives, or reprinted accounts, helps one to vicariously experience the plight of others, by seeing the world through their eyes.

Historical background is vital to understanding others, whether Native American, Hispanic, Mid-eastern, African or Asian. Teachers would do well to assign readings from source documents that help students emphasize with others. Students, fortified with a deeper knowledge of history, are then better equipped to bridge differences of other cultures.

Any study of history should be an honest quest for truth, including both positive and negative factors, allowing history to speak for itself without embellishment. We do not need to reconstruct history or fabricate to teach cultural lessons, and neither should we cover up events we wish had never happened. John Quincy Adams once wisely said that if we do not also face the unpleasant facts of history, we do not learn from our errors. The Christian community should be especially concerned about the lessons that can be learned from frank history for meaningful dialogue, so that we relate better to others for effective witnessing of our faith.

Find Models of Bridge Builders in History

While preparing classroom units of history, teachers should look to past rare individuals of vision who deserve to be singled out for being noble at a time when it was not always expedient to do so. Praise those courageous people who spoke for the victims of injustice. Many of them still have a message for today, and could well serve as models to be emulated. Among the following historical figures are many individuals worth assigning to students for research projects, and many who could also be incorporated into effective role-playing activities. There are Native Americans, like Chief Joseph, Powhatan and Blackhawk, whose eloquent speeches are so moving that they should be read aloud to be fully appreciated. The same could be said of the bridge builder Martin Luther King with his "I Had A Dream" speech delivered in the nation's capital. King wisely sought to bring all Americans together as a people, to be judged by their character and not by the color of their skin.

SPEAKING OUT

There also are noteworthy models of bridge builders among the Caucasians, like the New England minister John Elliot, the "Apostle to the Indians." His compassion for Native Americans and his love for the Gospel compelled him to speak against the larger Puritan society that apparently had wandered from its moral footings. Another voice that should still be heard is that of Episcopal Bishop Whipple of Minnesota. In 1862, while ministering to Native Americans, he sternly warned the government of Abraham Lincoln that the mistreatment of the Dakota was creating an explosive atmosphere. When hostilities broke out, General John Pope asked that the natives be treated as "maniacs or wild beasts". Standing out against this rush to judgment, Bishop Whipple interceded with President Lincoln. He was successful in earning a reprieve for all but 38 of the more than 300 captive natives who had been sentenced to death. Lincoln, too, stands out as a profile in courage for acting on behalf of helpless natives in the shadow of the hangman's noose. Lincoln was a compassionate soul in an age when the issue of race threatened the nation itself. Teachers might also identify more recent figures, like Hubert Humphrey, who in 1948 helped lead his party from bigotry into the fresh air of civil rights. There is no shortage of worthy examples that could be drawn upon.

Sometimes the heroes were not as well known as those mentioned above. The common frontier soldiers, who witnessed the slaughter of innocent Cheyenne men, women and children at the 1862 Sand Creek Massacre, had the courage to speak out against their commander Col. Chivington. This was hardly a popular stance on the Colorado frontier. The subsequent government hearings on the atrocity brought forth the detailed testimony of these soldiers, so that now this horrendous event may be a lesson of history. These bygone voices can also give courage to everyone to speak out against racism and injustice. There are numerous source books, with edited accounts like the above, in any local library.

RACE AND MULTICULTURALISM

Enhance Bridge Building by Personal Travel

Travel study tours for teachers and college students, or sometimes just planned travel, can make history come alive and promote a better understanding of minorities and those of different traditions. College study tours within the United States were conducted by DMLC for many years. One of the objectives of those tours was to give students exposure to other cultures outside their own circles. For example, tours included African-American civil rights sites in Memphis, Montgomery, Birmingham, Selma and Atlanta; Asian-American sites in the Chinatowns of San Francisco and New York City as well as Japanese-American relocation camps like Topaz in Utah; Hispanic sites in El Pueblo de Los Angeles and the famous California Mission Trail; and Native American sites at Pipestone, Wounded Knee, the Cherokee Trail of Tears and Apache Land in Arizona.

Through world travel, teachers can visit cultural settings that broaden outlooks on other cultural ways of life. At the same time, one becomes aware of the great gulf between the "haves" and "have-nots" in Third World nations. Teachers do well to place themselves in the not so accustomed position of being a minority in another culture. With an open mind, one can learn very much about others and see beauty and value in the unfamiliar. The more recent world travel experiences of Martin Luther College students in Europe, Turkey, Latin America and Africa have been invaluable in broadening their perspectives. When the college offered a study tour/safari in Kenya and Tanzania, the participants stepped into a world unlike anything they had known. At an African school in Arusha, they were invited to observe classroom instruction by dedicated teachers who had facilities quite unlike those in the United States. Afterwards the local teachers and students graciously treated the MLC students to traditional African songs and dances. The veteran teachers and future church workers on the tour gained immeasurably from this experience of bridge building. Opportunities for world travel continue to be available at MLC, sometimes in conjunction with

Bethany Lutheran College and Wisconsin Lutheran College. Teachers may check the MLC web site under Special Services (Professor John Paulsen) for current offerings.

Use Bridge Building Class Assignments

There are a number of interactive projects that could be devised for the benefit of students. The following example is only one suggestion for upper elementary grades or high school students. Divide the class into five or more groups and assign each group a regional U.S. area. Stress that students are to find information that relates to any ethnic or racial groups in their respective region. Have them search for museums, information centers, WELS missions, and cultural and historical sites pertaining to minorities. Instruct each regional group to subdivide themselves into states within their region. Individual students are then to use computers to locate free historic site information on their states, to use travel guides from the public library (or inter-library loan), to seek information from their parents and relatives, to phone or write their elected government officials (who have staff and access to government publications), to write to state historical societies for brochures, etc. Possibly the teacher could send out a memo to the parents asking to borrow personal copies of guidebooks like Frommers. AAA and Mobil Travel Guides. If you have history buffs in your congregation, you may even find *Macmillan's Monuments and Historic Places* or National Geographic's *American's Historical Places*. These books could be placed on a temporary reserve desk in the classroom for student use.

After a given time, perhaps six weeks, with the teacher having made periodic progress checks, have the students meet with their regional group to pool their information. Then direct each group to construct a regional map with significant site locations penciled in. Ask them to connect the sites with a line as if planning a trip. Then they may determine how many miles between the sites and how much time it would take between sites if they traveled a given rate of speed. If you wish to add a little more practical math, they could also determine the cost of gasoline required, using 20 miles per gallon at current prices. For even further activity, students could figure the number of days required for their hypothetical trip (estimating time spent at each site) and the most economical cost of overnight lodging by using the Expedia or Travelocity web sites.

A creative music teacher might teach each regional group an ethnic folk song suggested by their particular findings. Schedule a culminating activity with a Parent Teachers' Association meeting, or Open House, in which students explain their itineraries on posted regional maps and relate what might be learned from their virtual-reality trip. Students might be prevailed upon to even draw up travel posters, possibly as an art project, to entice "visitors" to explore their regions. This assignment incorporates computer and library skills, cooperative learning and cross curriculum work. If two classrooms are combined for the assignment, team teaching is also involved. Most importantly, the end result is learning about cultural diversity.

Build Bridges in Your Neighborhood

Teachers should find ways to make their students aware of the richness in cultural diversity within their own neighborhood. Help them locate members of their congregation or people in the community who are familiar with a foreign country and invite them to share their insights. A Lutheran school in Fort Worth, Texas had a lady from Japan plan and prepare a traditional Japanese meal, complete with chopsticks, for their noon meal. Such an activity could be timed with an origami art project or the planning of a Japanese garden.

Express a willingness to reach out in the neighborhood by enjoying festivals and holidays with those around you. Welcome the Chinese New Year. Have students celebrate Martin Luther King's Birthday and Black History Month in January. Wear green and walk in the St. Patrick's

Day parade with Irish-Americans in March. Think plaid on April 6th, National Tartan Day. Have a Mexican menu in your lunch program for Cinco de Mayo in May. Locate and attend a Pow Wow during Native American Heritage Month in November. Go out of your way to interact and extend the hand of friendship to people of other cultures wherever possible. Chances are the neighborhood will reciprocate. In all areas of WELS, we are coming in contact with Hispanics and the rich flavor of the Spanish language. Many of our Lutheran schools are now teaching Spanish, a great tool for building bridges. While we continue to cherish our own particular heritage, let us share it with others in this cultural exchange and appreciate whatever cultural diversity is present in our daily life experiences. When communication channels have been opened, we can better share our Christian faith, the ultimate act of kindness to our neighbors.

Some of us may not have a culturally diverse neighborhood or school. In that case, teachers should bring in resource people on a regular basis. Our congregations and schools could invite knowledgeable speakers to express their outlook and experiences and to share traditional artifacts. Within our WELS we have college and seminary professors who have personally served in the mission fields. Missionaries on furlough usually avail themselves of opportunities to tell others about their experiences. WELS teachers who have served in the Friends of China program in Beijing have fascinating experiences to share. Lutheran principals and teachers from schools in minority neighborhoods are often quite willing to visit other schools or church groups to build bridges. If possible include those who actually are of other cultures for an opportunity to personally interact with another race or culture. For a really edifying experience, teachers or congregations might invite the Voices of Praise Gospel Choir based at St. Marcus in Milwaukee to sing at their church or fellowship hall (Contact person: Rev. Mark Jeske). Another inspiring WELS Christian music group, replete with Latin American steel drum music is located at Hope Lutheran Church in Toronto, Canada (Contact person, Rev. Tom Haar). For information on Hmong culture or Friends of China, contact Rev. Loren Steele at Mt. Olive Lutheran Chinese Church in St. Paul, Minnesota.

Build Bridges Through Good Citizenship

As teachers and individual citizens, we can help promote a sense of fairness among minorities, government officials and ourselves. The quilt-like pattern of our nation makes up a single fabric called American. Differences of cultures have not weakened our nation; they have strengthened it. One of the factors that unite us is that we live in a nation under laws, which should respect and address the needs of all citizens. Because it is important that all citizens be served with wisdom and compassion, we need to encourage prayer for our nation and its government.

God clearly says in his Word that we should have respect for government, an ordinance of God, so that we can live together in harmony and tranquility. Our form of government may not be the only formula for government, but the United States Constitution is a time-proven document that serves well as a foundation for varying people to live together. The Founding Fathers took the best of British traditions, the wisdom of the French philosophes and the experience of colonial-self government to forge this document. Then it took great skill and leadership of statesmen, like John Dickinson, to build bridges among thirteen sovereign and independent states to ratify this document. To appreciate these accomplishments, one has to understand the historical context of this difficult bridge building. The Constitution served as a bridge among factions, and as Jefferson had hoped, with amendments it improved with time. The first ten amendments provided for individual rights and following amendments expanded those rights to others. Eventually civil rights legislation of the 1960s filled in more of the gaps. Teachers can emphasize to their students that citizens and voters have an obligation to influence their government in a positive way to better serve all segments of its citizenry.

SPEAKING OUT

Acknowledge the Ultimate Bridge Builder

Since God made all people of one blood, we really are, in a sense, all brothers and sisters in the human family. Christ died for all of races, all ethnic backgrounds and us. Every one of us are sinners that have been redeemed by the Sacrifice on the cross. Our Lord is the ultimate Bridge Builder, not only in this world but also leading to the next. May we, as sanctified Christians, fully appreciate all people of all cultures. Pray for tolerance and understanding in our regular classroom witnessing, that we may all sit together at the Heavenly Feast God has prepared for us.

> Lord of all nations, grant me grace
> To love all people, every race,
> And in each person help me view
> My kindred, loved, redeemed by you.
>
> Break down the wall that would divide
> Your children, Lord on every side.
> My neighbors' good let me pursue;
> Bind them to me and all to you.
>
> CW 521: 1-2

Share Your Bridge Building Ideas with Others

Other teachers might be interested in what you are doing, or have done, in your school and congregations to effectively handle cultural diversity. If you wish to share your own experiences or ideas, please e-mail your responses to the undersigned.

Frederick Wulff (fredwulff@newulmtel.net)
Retired MLC professor residing in New Ulm

RACE AND MULTICULTURALISM

POLITICAL CORRECTNESS MADNESS

Originally written as a Letter to the Minneapolis Star Tribune *2012, but not submitted*

A letter to the Editor in Friday's morning's edition of the *Star Tribune* made an interesting comment about beer brewed in New Ulm called Nordeast. That contributor believed that name could offend residents of Northeast Minneapolis. It seems like there is no end to how people use offensive words. Have you ever wondered how white Southerners must cringe when they go a supermarket and see an aisle sign with the word "Crackers"? According to the 1911 edition of the Encyclopedia Britannica, it is a term of contempt for the "poor" or "mean whites," particularly of Georgia and Florida. If one goes down the cracker aisle there are Saltine Crackers, Oyster Crackers, Graham Crackers and even Crushed Crackers. Then we see Cracker Barrel Restaurants -- and every 4th of July Fire Crackers are advertised on billboards. There is no end to the hurt. It is enough to make a person turn to drink. Southern Comfort should fit the bill. Oops, sorry about that to all you Bills out there. Take time out and have a beer!

Fred Wulff, New Ulm

WE NEED A "CONVERSATION"

Letter to the Editor New Ulm Journal *August 2, 2013*

The Dangers of Balkanization

Our country is being Bulkanized by those who seize on the Travon Martin – George Zimmermann case to further divide us into racial categories. History reveals many examples how sharp divisions can tear a nation apart. Daily news reports coming in from around the world echo the same message. I believe that many of those leaders who are calling for Zimmermann's blood are rehashing an old battle from the 50s and 60s. To make Zimmerman fear for his life, because one of his parents was white, makes no sense.

Past Injustices

Some activists keep picking at the scabs of the past and refuse to allow healing to take place. Their memories of an unjust era still lingers. I too recall vividly those old days and they were ugly. When my parents moved us to Texas in the late 40s we were shocked at the terrible treatment of people based only on skin color. In every phase of life, even in churches, minorities were humiliated. Fortunately this evil was put on the public agenda by both blacks and whites that courageously sacrificed themselves to show the country (and the world) just how unjust racial discrimination is, and how brutal the oppressors could be in defending that institution. We as a nation had a lot to learn.

Progress

Has there been progress or does the Zimmermann verdict show nothing has changed? I submit significant changes have been made. Acts have been passed by Congress to enfranchise blacks and ensure rights. Government officials such as a former Chairman of the Joint Chiefs of Staff, a former Secretary of State, the present President and his Attorney General, as well as the Director of the ATF, are black. Clearly college campuses overwhelmingly support minority rights. Black studies are among the courses taught. I belonged to the Organization of American Historians for thirty years and I can attest to the fact that minority views dominated the agendas of annual conferences. I challenge anyone to point out unfavorable views of minorities in the textbooks used in our schools. Actually, the slant is quite the opposite, and has been for the last thirty years. Our country doesn't need to apologize to the world, as the major media outlets would suggest.

Conversation With Solutions

Do problems still exist? Yes, but I suggest minorities seek new leaders who have a vision for the future and seek reconciliation. Those seeking an individual case to enflame the public to demonstrate and destroy property does not serve the public interest. No enforcement agency will ever be entirely free of losers. A fresh approach would look at the real problems of disparity. Instead of just offering excuses and ignoring serious neighborhood problems, we need to dig a little deeper for solutions. We all know the heartbreaking statistics that stifle the achievement of the young. The conversation might begin with how the victim mentally is by its nature self defeating. Mrs. Obama had it right when she once told black school children that she is an example of how they too can make it. Good parenting, a stable family, possibly charter schools and decent role models worth emulating, might make good talking points. It would also be helpful for any constructive conversation to avoid the labeling of a different viewpoint as racist.

Frederick Wulff, retired

HEALING THAT HEALS

LETTER TO THE EDITOR
New Ulm *Journal*, November 10, 2002

Claims of an Activist

An article on the front page of the New Ulm *Journal* (Saturday, November 9) about Native Americans had a subheading "SSU professor says Hitler patterned torture after U.S. genocide techniques." This was followed with the assertion Hitler studied, admired and patterned his torture techniques after those used on Native Americans in the 1862 Dakota conflict. I question that any speeches, writings or correspondence of Hitler refer to his studying Minnesota history of the Civil

War era and thus being inspired to practice genocide. Nor am I aware of any noted scholar of German history ever making such a statement about Hitler in the context of the Minnesota conflict.

The same article goes on to note that this SSU professor who spoke at Turner Hall drew parallels between Hitler's Nazi German concentration camps with Mankato and Fort Snelling. This is outrageous. There is no doubt the Dakota were abused and mistreated and their story is a dark chapter in Minnesota history. For that matter, the suffering was quite universal in America for the natives as westward expansion deprived them of their land, threatening both livelihood and culture, and taking a toll of lives in defensive warfare. When I researched my doctoral dissertation on Native Americans, I came to develop a strong empathy for these people. I am heartened by the fact that leading American historians like Horsman, Prucha, Edmunds and others have published scholarly works that point out the harshness in which these people were treated and the injustices they have endured. The Native Americans do not need wild and inaccurate comparisons for their cause. Truthful history is on their side.

The SSU professor goes on to say "we are still trying to heal." According to the account it appears that this is to be accomplished by finding and passing down stories such as sick Dakota crying as they were scalded with hot water by white people. Using this same logic I suppose I could bring healing to German-American people who are descendants of the New Ulm settlers by recounting and dwelling on individual atrocities allegedly committed against them.

Need for Efforts that Heal

Rather, to heal, I suggest we follow the example of Martin Luther College, which hosted a conference for Native Americans on the MLC campus last year as a gesture of reconciliation. This invitation not only promoted emotional healing; the subject of the conference, combating diabetes among Native Americans, fostered physical healing. I commend our honorable mayor Arnold Koelpin who addressed the gathering at Turner Hall last Friday and acknowledged the Native American cultural heritage. He did so in a spirit of respect as he did 17 months ago at the Summer Institute at Martin Luther College.

When New Ulm first hosted its Heritagefest celebration in 1975, a great effort was made by the promoters to involve the Native Americans. The Heritage Pageant, the main event at that time, was set up to include the Dakota and to sympathetically and accurately portray their plight during the 1862 conflict. My wife was chairperson of the costume committee at the time and I know that she met with a number of our Dakota neighbors from Morton for advice and participation. Most of the Native Americans I know favor this kind of reconciliation, not inflammatory rhetoric that further divides us.

Need for Better Spokespersons

Finally, if Native Americans still feel hurt from "the painful memories of New Ulm" and "are very reluctant to visit New Ulm," as stated in the article, it may be because some individuals, like the SSU speaker, will not let the wounds heal because they persist in rubbing the sores to keep them open. They may mean well and work with zeal. I appreciate their concerns. These people make sensational speakers at national and international conferences with their politically correct oratory, but what the Native Americans really need are bridge builders to the future. The Dakota are good and proud people who deserve healing that really heals.

Frederick Wulff, New Ulm

SPEAKING OUT

LETTER TO THE EDITOR: RESPONSE TO THE RESPONSE: HEALING THAT REALLY HEALS

Commemorative Marches Are Beneficial

I appreciate the Southwest State Professor Numpa responding to my letter to the editor. First, it was helpful to get a more comprehensive report of what transpired at the Turner Hall meeting of November 9th. We could all have benefited from fuller treatment of what was said by other participants. Secondly, I was pleased to hear of the greeting you received from our community, being fed and housed and such. New Ulm is a friendly community to visitors and I'm glad you were accorded such hospitality. As did your hosts, I support the concept of your commemorative march, and if I had known about it would have probably marched with you. I share your desire to mark the 1862 historic march of history. That event reminded me of the Long March by Native Americans to Washington DC in the late 1970s. I still recall a rally in Milwaukee, which my family attended, where activist Clyde Bellecourt personally sold "Long March" T-shirts to my daughters. The history of Native Americans is an integral part of our nation's history and it should be remembered.

Poor Analogy with Holocaust

I still question the wisdom of your Nazi concentration camp analogy. Concentration camps in the generic sense of the word can well be used in a number of situations, but we all know the horrors of the Holocaust. As bad as the incarceration of the Native Americans was, the Nazi parallel is overdrawn. Your source for the Hitler "quote" was not really a quotation, but a generalization from a secondary account. That account for " one of your favorite comments," came from the book *American Holocaust: Columbus and the Conquest of the New World* by David E. Stannard. His basic premise is that Christianity provided the ideology for the genocide just as it provided the ideology for the Nazi Holocaust. I would argue that a secular society, called Christian, promulgated the injustices done in both cases. The Christianity of the Bible surely does not condone such things. An added note: Historian Russell Thornton (University of California, Berkeley) says that Stannard's book "occasionally surpasses the bounds of knowledge." He also says the metaphor of holocaust is carried too far. "Stannard views population decline solely in the context of genocide. But colonialism and its impact on Native American population did not always equal genocide."

No, you are not alone in your above interpretation. I am personally sensitive to a Balkanization approach of some militants. I hate to see research and scholarship take a back seat to sensational emotionalism, and for civilized debate to degenerate into charged rhetoric. I have seen too often where academics are called racist because their findings do not always fit into a prescribed politically correct mold. The sad part of all of this is that legitimate concerns for minorities can be sacrificed by the divisiveness.

Need for Tempered Statements

None of my relatives were colonizers. I really don't think of myself as Euroamerican, but as an American. All of my grandparents were born in Germany so none of them were in America in the nineteenth century to subjugate Native Americans. Because we have white skin does that mean that we are racist and incapable of making comments about history? When my daughter attended Southwest State she did not encounter such "rancorous" expressions. We have differences of opinion, but I did not charge you with being racist. I expressed my opinion that individuals like yourself were "well meaning and zealous," but that your comments hurt the cause of Native Americans. I don't give speeches and I may not be a spokesperson for New Ulm, but I still believe relations between the races can be accomplished (healing that really heals) with more tempered comments than those you made at the Turner Hall.

Frederick Wulff

New Ulm

LETTER TO THE EDITOR: BIPOLARIZING NATIVE AMERICAN HISTORY

One could argue that this dialogue on Native Americans is being overdone, but Professor Chris Mato Nunpa has made a good point that now the readers have a chance to see the difference between perspectives. He notes it is good for these issues to be discussed to inform the public. Citizens should be informed about what is being taught in their tax supported universities. Professor Nunpa is correct again when he states there is an emerging new perspective in opposition to the Euroamerican framework. This is increasingly obvious at professional conferences. Recently, I heard a speaker vigorously applauded by fellow professors at a major conference for denouncing the United States Constitution "as a white man's document". This comment was made after the chairman for the National Endowment for the Humanities had suggested that the Constitution could be the basis for consensus. Euroamericanism was put on the defensive.

One could disagree, however, when Professor Chris Mato Nunpa infers that an indigenous perspective of Native Americans is synonymous to his Nazi Concentration Camp Holocaust theory. There is merit in an indigenous perspective and learning from Native American teachers. As part of one of my doctoral language requirements, in lieu of learning the Shawnee language, I participated in a University of Wisconsin live-in seminar. For six weeks I (and my family) lived off the land in secluded woodland of Wisconsin. All of my instructors were friendly and knowledgeable Native Americans: John Boatman (Ojibwe), Irene

Mack (Menomonee), Wallace Pyawasit (Menomonee/Potawatomi), Keewaydinoquay Ph.D. (Ojibwe) Lillian Rice (Chippewa/Escanaba) and James Zhuckkahosee (Kickapoo). The advisor for my dissertation was part Shawnee. This professor did look Euroamerican, and he may even have been "tainted" by Christianity, but he had some Native American blood. None of these "indigenous" people above used the Holocaust paradigm advocated by Professor Numpa. My research in the National Archive of Canada in Ottawa brought me in contact with many original documents that had been written by Native Americans. A person can be a Euroamerican, even a Christian, and yet be an informed student of Native American history. The current partitioning of "we" vs Euroamericans is artificial and harmful. Underneath the color of our skins we are all members of the human family, made of one blood to dwell on this earth.

Frederick Wulff
New Ulm

LETTER FROM A DAKOTA, JOHN LA BATTE TO FREDERICK WULFF

December 16, 2002

Dear Mr. Wulff,

I am writing to say that I fully agree with your recent comments in the New Ulm *Journal*.

I am familiar with Mr. Mato Numpa (nee Chris Cavender). I have heard him speak and have read his articles. I don't agree with his message. I am descended from hostile and innocent Dakota Indians who were involved in the Dakota Conflict. He doesn't speak for my ancestors. Given the low participation in the "march", he doesn't speak for very many others.

I feel Mr. Mato Nunpa staged this march to advance his personal agenda than to "remember and honor the 1700 Dakota people." I don't understand why he and a very few others want to keep the hate and anger alive. They hate their white ancestors for what they did to their Indian ancestors.

I am not as widely read as you and Mr. Mato Numpa, but will match my knowledge of the Dakota Indians and the Dakota Conflict with anyone.

In 1862, following the trials, two groups of Indians departed from the Lower Sioux Agency. All Indians who were tried (about 350) were taken to Mankato by way of New Ulm. At least two of my ancestors were in this group. The other group (about 1700 innocent Indians) crossed the Minnesota River and traveled to Fort Snelling by way ay of Fort Ridgely and Henderson. At least 5 of my ancestors were in this group. Mr. Mato Numpa states that it was one march of 150 miles. The route from Lower Sioux to Fort Snelling was about 120 miles. The Commemorative March was not historically correct in its route or its numbers.

Recently, I came across a New Ulm newspaper article describing an 1892 New Ulm observance of the Battles of New Ulm. Over 20,000 people attended. Indians were invited. They attended and participated. Reconciliation and forgiveness had already started in 1892. I think there was a ceremony at Fort Ridgely regarding this. Mr. Mato Numpa stated "the United States, Minnesota and its Euroamerican citizenry are in denial big-time." I don't believe this.

There is much more that can be said about this and other comments made by Mr. Mato Numpa. I will deal with this one day. I gave 2 speeches in New Ulm in August at the Brown County Museum about my Dakota Ancestors. I spoke to high school kids in New Ulm and Sleepy this past fall. I plan to move to New Ulm in the spring and hope to continue my efforts to get the true story out through speeches, written articles and a web site.

I visit New Ulm every few weeks. If you wish to discuss this further, perhaps we can meet.

Sincerely,
John LaBatte

Dear John La Batte,

Thank you for your very kind letter and comments about my letters to the editor of the Journal.

I appreciate all that you do to further the cause of the Dakota. I look forward to reading the book you are currently working on. My wife has heard you speak in New Ulm. I was also impressed that you spoke to the New Ulm Sr. High School class recently. I'm sending along a page from *Focus 88* that has an article (and picture) about you.

I was out of state in 1987 during the Year of Reconciliation so did not hear you at that commemoration. You may have met one of my teachers from the University of Wisconsin who spoke at Fort Ridgley and in New Ulm for the occasion. His name is Reginald Horsman. He was my advisor for my master's thesis on Shawnee Indians and he guided me to a topic on the Shawnee for my doctoral dissertation with R.

David Edmunds (now at the University of Indiana).

I hope you do not mind if I submit your name to the Lyceum Director of Martin Luther College as a possible speaker. Before I retired I was the director and sought out Native Americans as speakers. You are a valuable resource!

We could all benefit more from a study of Native Americans.

Sincerely,

Frederick Wulff

CONFERENCE: MULTICULTURAL HISTORY AND THE NATIVE AMERICANS

Presentation by Frederick Wulff to the WELS Lutheran High School Conference, Wisconsin Lutheran College, October 24, 1991

PART I Christians teachers should give adequate treatment to Native Americans

Christian "Correctness"

Christian teachers must look beyond their own culture to give their students sympathetic insights into their multicultural communities. We are on this earth to proclaim God's message of salvation to all people. We must be sensitive to others who have a culture different from our own. Our cultural differences should not be a stumbling block in our teaching ministry. This will require a deliberate effort if we are to be truly successful. We may feel less secure and comfortable in a setting where we recognize other "social realities" than our traditional one, but our true security and comfort do not come from cultural traditions. Our ultimate reference point is God's Word, which transcends cultural differences.

Our Christian integrity would compel us to be fair and honest in our treatment of others, both in the presentation of the past and in our treatment of the present. We must attempt to give others their rightful place in history and in society.

What better opportunity is there in our curriculum for becoming acquainted with and for respecting other cultures than when we teach social studies? Given that our schools and communities are fast becoming multicultural, our approach must be multicultural. Fortunately, we no longer have the label of having the "German schools". Even if we have no Native Americans in our immediate classrooms, we in the Midwest have sizeable Native American communities around us, either in urban neighborhoods or on reservations. We also have close Synodical ties with our Apache brothers and sisters in Arizona. Let's be more sensitive to Native American culture. To treat others and their cultures with fairness and objectivity is compatible with Christianity. We do well to do unto others, as we would have them do unto us.

Political "Correctness"

The multicultural approach does not necessarily mean we have to deny our own cultural debts to Europe. I believe it is true that here in the United States we do have strong cultural debts to Europe - to the heritage of western civilization. I confess that in my history lectures at DMLC I stress cherished political roots and constitutional developments that have come mainly from English traditions. Some may argue that this approach is currently not in vogue, or not "politically correct," but I disagree. I also believe that the Christian mission efforts from Europe were a blessing to this nation, and that those who did mission work among the Indians were not all uncaring or insensitive people. It may be "politically correct" to denounce early Christian missionaries and to make sport of them, but they deserve fair objective treatment, too. In retrospect we now see the errors of these churchmen as they worked among Indians. Clearly errors were made; but the sincere motives of these missionaries and the personal hardships they endured should not be overlooked. Cultural baggage interfered with their efforts and no doubt they could have profited from a multicultural orientation. However, the message of salvation they preached was really the Water of Life needed by all people, including the Indians. Arthur Schlesinger, Jr. recently expressed his fear of the attack on the "Eurocentric" curriculum. He was concerned that "Europe - the unique source of the liberating ideas of democracy, civil liberties, and human rights - is portrayed as the root of all evil." (See "The Cult of Ethnicity, Good and God," *Time*, July 8, 1991.). I share some of his concerns. I will have to concur also with Professor Theodore Hartwig when he stated in his 1990 symposium address "the story of western civilization is essential for knowing ourselves, our own institutions, our own way of life."

Yet at the same time we must recognize the need for a multicultural vision that includes other cultural influences. We Americans, though of various ethnic groups, are all Americans. I think we all agree there is a need to present a more balanced account, a broader view of history, rather than a too simplistic view that ignores the varied influences of others. The Lord has brought people here from many lands, including the early "Indians" from Asia, and the flow of immigrants from other lands is still taking place. Our country is a mosaic of different cultures, and in this modern age we are becoming more and more mindful that we are citizens of the world. Americans are quite multicultural. Americans are increasingly marrying across ethnic and racial lines. Our neighborhoods and congregations are becoming multicultural. The current trend in our nation toward a multicultural approach to history is, therefore, a healthy trend. It is a strong movement and merits our serious attention.

To be sure the multicultural approach has its critics who fear such teaching will cost us our social cohesion. But people of other cultures have made an impact on this nation and their influence and contributions should not be slighted. If we have Native Americans, or Blacks, or Hispanics in our schools, churches, and neighborhoods we can actually strengthen our unity by acknowledging and seeking to understand the various contributions of these groups. We will be richer for it. And among the peoples we surely would want to include are the very people who inhabited our land before Europeans even dreamed there was a new world.

Historical "Correctness"

Native Americans deserve considerable treatment in our history classes and they deserve to be treated with respect. In the past they have been maligned, or at best ignored. It is historically correct to say these first Americans have been the victims of abuse from ambitious incursions into their lands. Historian John Garraty of Columbia University reminds us: "Don't forget the most flagrant example of unprovoked aggression in human history." We who teach history should be unflinchingly honest. As Christians, especially as Christian teachers, we want to be as truthful and honest as possible. We respect truth simply because it is truth. John Quincy Adams understood that American historians could all too easily write a nationalistic history that overlooked, explained away, or sugarcoated past misbehavior. Adams insisted that a good historian "has no country." He added: "For otherwise, how can a country profit and learn salutary lessons from past error?" (*OAH Newsletter*, February 1988).

Earlier history textbooks have often been blatantly unfair to American Indians. Fortunately the sixties and the seventies were years when more objective and scholarly works came out on Native Americans. Much of this can be attributed to increasing awareness of "minorities. With the civil rights movements came more sensitivity toward minorities. Old entrenched ideas and stereotyped images, however, continue to plague us. Bias and prejudice against people like Native Americans still exists.

SPEAKING OUT

Cultural "Correctness"

Do we ourselves harbor feelings that Native Americans are lesser or inferior people than we? Do we have hearts filled with prejudice? Are we patronizing or condescending when we teach about other cultures? No doubt our WELS has many spirit filled students and teachers who strive to free themselves from bigotry or prejudice or a condescending attitude. Yet, from my experience of twenty years of teaching at DMLC, I would have to say that I have heard students express negative feelings about Indians and "their ways". Some students have even resented the class time allotted to the role of Indians in history. I have also heard the statement: "Why study Indians? We are not Indians!" Perhaps students see the early Native Americans as less important because some tribes were less complex in social structure and organization than we are familiar with. A case could be made that the Native Americans have cultural traditions that are not "inferior". Some characteristics that anthropologists and historians attribute to Native Americans are worthy of emulation, such as respect for the environment, non-materialism, a spirit of freedom and independence and close kinship ties. (Note the positive tone of an attached 10/13/91 article from the *Minneapolis Star Tribune*: "Indian Ways Inspire Children to Love the Earth."

As Lutherans we naturally cherish our own ethnic heritage. There is nothing wrong with that. Actually, to know and to appreciate your roots and customs makes your life richer. Perhaps though, this brings about an ethnocentrism that obscures a broader understanding of others. This may be a bigger problem for us Lutherans than for those who live with a greater mixture of nationalities. Our students, and even we teachers, may judge others only by our culture, from our own narrow perspective. We treasure our Biblical value system, and rightly so. We do not want to question God's norms. However, there are areas of culture that remain relative. Other cultures differ from ours, but they are not necessarily inferior because they are unlike our own. We need to be aware of the need for objectivity in the study of history and culture of the Native Americans. God created these people and permitted them the honor of being the first inhabitants of this land -- to be the First Americans. The Native American culture is worthy of study.

Pre-history "Correctness"

That the Indians, including the Aluts and Eskimos, came originally from Asia is now almost universally accepted. These people began coming over in Old Testament times and had established diverse cultures, well before any Europeans in the New World.

Now that our nation is giving much attention to the 500th anniversary of the expedition of Christopher Columbus, we have great opportunities to bring in the Native Americans who were there to greet him. See newspaper article "A Year to Discover Rich History of the Very First Americans" in the appendix. When we begin our study of the New World, we should have our students seek an understanding of these people as they were before the West intruded upon their lives. By taking this approach, students may gain a greater sense of the changes that occurred, both good and bad, after Christopher Columbus landed at San Salvador. A study of this kind will likely bring out the wide variety found among the various tribes in the New World. If we divide our class into small groups, each assigned to explore different pre-Columbian cultures (Aztecs, Incas, Navahos, Anasasi, Mississippians of Cahokia, etc.), this would help bring out the richness and diversity prevalent among the tribes. This assignment could be easily carried out with issues of past National Geographic magazines. All of the above pre-Columbian cultures have received considerably attention by anthropologists and archeologists and the listing of related articles can be easily found in the *National Geographic* index volumes.

True we lack written records of these people before the Europeans came here, but much can be learned about these people through archeological ruins and oral traditions. When we plan high school class trips we might include Cahokia, Illinois to study the mound Indians who had developed a massive community and trade center just east of St. Louis. Teachers who intend to visit St. Louis on a field trip could very easily stop at Cahokia en route since it is right off the Interstate. Possibly your choir tours or band excursions that travel into the southwest could schedule stops at Pueblo dwellings in Arizona and New Mexico -- or better yet the Mesa Verde in southwestern Colorado. Our DMLC travel study tours found all of the above sites worthwhile visiting

Seek Scholarly Authors

Native Americans have experienced a "bad press" in the past that we should try to correct with the help of more recent studies. Since the Native Americans did not have a written language, latecomers from Europe wrote the first historical accounts only from the white man's viewpoint. The Indians were naturally relegated to the role of savages or just simply a topic for romantic literature. Later historians did little better using one-sided sources in one-sided historical accounts. Textbooks, until recently, introduced us to the American scene by starting with the European incursion. Some historians chose to ignore the Indians or to treat them as a problem encountered by settlers. Frontier historian Frederick Jackson Turner failed to appreciate these people. Turner celebrated the 400th anniversary of 1492 a century ago with his famous essay on how the frontier keeps recreating "new worlds "overcoming the "savages"" who originally were there. Historians who look at the records will find evidence that "savages" on the frontier were whites as well as Indians. All people of all races have a sinful nature and all groups of people have their element of excess. But surely if historians looking for objectivity seek to find "savages" and savage behavior they will not come down one-sided against those who were defending their homelands and a way of life. I believe that recent books by authors like Wilcomb Washburn, Reginald Horsman, R. David Edmunds and the like are a healthy remedy to previous misconceptions. Sensitive treatment of Indians can also be found in a timely film release "Dances With Wolves". Here Indians are treated as real people and as people with a real culture.

If you would like a very readable single volume paperback on the American Indian I would recommend *The Indian in America* by Wilcomb Washburn (Harper and Row, The *New American Nation Series*, 1975, ISBN 0-06-096436-4). According to the preface, "this volume seeks to give a general impression of the character and experiences of the many tribes and nations of the New World before, during, and after the shattering impact of their involvement with European settlers and their descendants." Book reviews from historians have been quite favorable. Alden Vaughan concedes that some specialists may challenge some of Washburn's generalizations, "but few readers, if any, will deny that *The Indian in America* is the best volume on the subject"

There is no shortage of qualified historians who are well versed on Indians. One of the nation's best historians on frontier Indians is Reginald Horsman of the University of Wisconsin-Milwaukee. Those of you who are in the Milwaukee area might consider taking a graduate course from professor Horsman. You might also enroll in a course with Francis Prucha of Marquette University. He is a leading frontier historian and has written many books on white/native American relations.

Possibly you may spring yourselves free to attend the forthcoming (November 7-9, 1991) Indian cultural conference at the Radisson Inn---Green Bay where various scholars from around the nation will discuss topics relating to Indian culture and history. Guided tours of the Wisconsin Oneida reservation will be available. See the appendix for more information on this conference.

SPEAKING OUT

Experience Native American Culture

One of the best ways to study Native American culture is to experience it. What better way to gain an Indian perspective than to live outdoors in a natural setting and have all of your instructors be Indians who teach you traditional Indian ways. I heartily recommend such a hands on experience. Back in 1978 I enrolled in a six-week live-in seminar offered by the University of Wisconsin. (See appendix for program cover.) Since the University attempted to create a natural Indian community in the "wilds" of northern Wisconsin, we were required to park our cars and campers elsewhere and to pitch a tent in the woods. More ambitious students chose to construct their own wigwams. The seminar directors encouraged us to bring our wives and children to create a natural village setting. One lady even brought her goat. Over fifty of us, including some Indian students, participated. We made our own medicine, gathered plants for food and teas, cooked meals on an open fire, built a canoe, made baskets of birch bark, constructed our own moccasins, learned Indian dances and customs, and so on. Our family learned firsthand that Indians are people who could teach us a lot - including humility.

If you are interested in this kind of activity you might check with Professor John Boatman (Ojibwe Indian) at UWM to see when the live-in seminar will be offered again as a summer course. UWM has a strong American Indian Studies program to acquaint all kinds of students with the American Indian heritage. John Boatman's phone number at UWM is 414-229-6686. The American Indian Studies department is located in rooms 181 and 179 of Holton Hall on the UWM campus.

A good way for you and your students to become a little better acquainted with Indians is to attend an Indian pow-wow in your area. The Menominee Indians of Wisconsin often host pow-wows in Menominee county. Of course there are many others. In the state of

Minnesota the Dakota nations meet annually in Mankato for three days of festivities. These pow-wows are open to the public. The last one offered in September of this year was attended by about forty of my DMLC students. When you as a teacher express an interest in Indian ways, you are helping to cultivate understanding and good will toward the culture of Native Americans. Usually pow-wows have exhibits of Indian artwork and crafts as well as food stands that may have Indian fare such as fry bread. Students will enjoy the music set to a drumbeat and the rhythmic dances. Some pow-wows, such as the ones in Mankato, encourage visitors to join in the dances, most of which are easily learned by simple observation.

Use Native American Sources

Go to the sources. I think students would profit from reading accounts of Indians found in various anthologies. Have students read some of their speeches aloud and have them try to visualize the setting and the emotions that prompted the speeches. There are a number of really moving speeches. Your class might try Chief Logan's Lament of 1774, which Thomas Jefferson offered as proof "of the talents of the aborigines of this country, and particularly of their eloquence." Or, Chief Seattle's Oration of 1854, often referred to as the "swan song" of his people. Both of these speeches may be found in *The American Reader*, a multicultural anthology of history and literature edited by Diane Ravitch (Harper, 1990). Better yet, you might want to select readings from *Great Documents in American Indian History*, edited by Wayne Moquin (Praeger Publishers, 1974, Library of Congress number 72-80583). This book contains not only famous speeches, eyewitness accounts to historical events and interviews, but also statements on the Indian hunting activity, family life, courtship and marriage, and the creation legends.

Introduce yourself, and your students, to books with personal accounts by Native Americans. Since many of you are from Wisconsin you might want to have your students read *The Autobiography of a Winnebago Indian* by Paul Radin (Library of Congress number 63-17914), or *Mountain Wolf Woman, Sister of Crashing Thunder*, the Autobiography of a Winnebago Indian edited by Nancy Lurie (ISBN 0-472-06109-7 paperbound). These Winnebago Indians were from Black River Falls, Wisconsin. Mountain Wolf Woman is especially interesting since it relates Indian life from a feminine perspective. Try to have your students see life from another's moccasins.

If we have Native Americans available to use as resource persons we should tap that source. Ask these Indians if they would be willing to share their knowledge of Indian language, music, dances, food recipes, artwork, or reservation life. Public speakers from Indian communities are often available for engagements. A number of our schools might pool resources to obtain speakers such as tribal chairman David Larson of the Lower Sioux reservation in Minnesota. This year he has been giving a presentation "1862, the Dakota Conflict." A group of teachers might want to form a car pool to hear well-known Indian leaders like Clyde Bellecourt when they speak at nearby cities. I heard Bellecourt speak at evening meetings at both Mankato State University and the University of Wisconsin in Milwaukee. Clyde Bellecourt, one of the founders of AIM, now serves the government as an advisor in Native American education and is knowledgeable on Indian Survival Schools.

Use Biographies of Native American Leaders

Students are often fascinated with the lives of Americans. Why not acquaint them with the lives of some Indian leaders (including Red Bird, a Winnebago of Wisconsin)? R. David Edmunds has edited a paperback: *Studies in Diversity, American Indian Leaders* (ISBN 0-8032-6705-3pbk), which includes twelve leaders or Indians of influence. Students will not be familiar with all of the leaders, although they may recognize some names like Joseph Brant, John Ross and Sitting Bull. We may want to observe days of commemoration for individuals or events in Native American history and possibly develop a teaching unit for the occasion. We could construct a documentary on the Cherokee Trail of Tears, the plight of Chief Joseph, the life and times of Chief Osceola, etc. The events might be depicted by a series of drawings or reenactments.

Use State and Federal Sources

A good source of information on Native Americans is from your state government or state historical society. Study the history and present status of tribes within your own state. Each state has an agency of some kind that puts out information booklets. Have students locate the reservations and find former treaty lines (see appendix attached for Wisconsin and Minnesota). Note the economy of the reservations, health problems, average income, etc. The students may then understand why the Wisconsin Commission on Human rights concluded: "Bound by generations of poverty, the Indians have met the deafening defeat of the spirit which joblessness and paternalism bring." The following booklets may be helpful for Wisconsin and Minnesota:

> *Handbook on Wisconsin Indians*, published with the cooperation of the University of Wisconsin Extension, 1966, compiled and written by Joyce M. Erdman, Governor's Commission on Human Rights, Madison, Wisconsin. Library of Congress 66.64334

> *Wisconsin Indians*, published by the State Historical Society of Wisconsin in Madison, 1982, compiled by Nancy Oestreich Lurie. E787.W817 977.600497 ISBN 0-87020-195-6

> *Indians in Minnesota*, published by the League of Women Voters, 1974, North Central Publishing Company in St. Paul. Library of Congress 77-169118 E78.M7 L37

All of the above conclude with selected references or reading list.

Use Classroom Activities

If you are looking for classroom activities you may find the following book from British Columbia helpful: *The NESA Activities Handbook for Native and Multicultural Classrooms* by Don Sawyer and Howard Green (ISBN 088978-186-9pbk). According to the authors "the games focus on and develop attitudes necessary for multicultural awareness and sensitivity." They believe these experiential exercises can lead to considerably social awareness and can have significant impact on attitudes. Each activity is introduced with stated goals, group size, time required, grade level and materials needed. Procedures are then outlined and followed by debriefing questions. The twenty-four exercises all extend to grade twelve. The first given are for grades one through twelve; the last ones are for high school grades only.

Use Current Events

Have your students discuss current event situations that involve Native Americans. Here in states like Wisconsin and Minnesota we often find articles in the daily newspapers about conflicts between area residents and Native Americans over local issues. Often racism is a major part of the issue. Before you begin a topic ask the student to think about the situation from the perspective of the Indians, area residents, the government and outsiders. The instructor could use a debate format. No doubt you have seen recent Associated Press newspaper articles about Indian religious practices and peyote (AP, "Indians want protection for peyote use, New Ulm *Journal*, p. 7A. September 22, 1991), the renaming of the Custer Battlefield National Monument to the Little Bighorn Battlefield (Scripps Howard News Service, *Star Tribune*, July 26, 1991), bingo casinos, spear fishing under treaty rights, mineral and lumber resources on Indian land, toxic waste disposal sites on Indian land, etc. Some of these issues are also treated from an Indian perspective in *Great*

RACE AND MULTICULTURALISM

Documents in American Indian History, edited by Wayne Moquin. The problems are often extremely complex and your discussion may end up inconclusive, but encourage your students to be sensitive toward others, to avoid stereotypes and quick prejudgments. As a follow-up assignment have students do writing assignments in which they are to seek reasonable possibly solutions to the issues whereby both harmony and justice are achieved.

Use Scripture

Our sinful nature makes it easy to become self-centered or to develop negative stereotypes of people from other races or ethnic background. We as Christian teachers will want to help students develop a Christ-like attitude towards others. Finally, Scripture is the best and most effective teaching aid we can use to help.

BOOK REVIEW: Hank H. Cox, *Lincoln and the Sioux Uprising of 1862* (Cumberland Press, Nashville, 2005) by Frederick Wulff, fredwulff@newulmtel.net

This book is timely. Just about everyone today seems interested in reading about cultural conflicts. Social studies teachers especially will appreciate this book because it rightly gives Lincoln credit for the courage to spare the lives of many Indians slated for execution for alleged crimes in the Uprising of 1862. Hank Cox attempts to fill the void on this subject. Although he does not unveil anything shockingly new, he does help the reader to understand the political pressure Lincoln elicited from the rabid Minnesota press which demanded swift "justice" for those Indian captives charged of capital crimes. In this heated climate, General Pope called for extermination of "the wild beasts." The settlers of Minnesota clamored for mass executions. Many of those aroused were voters that Lincoln sorely needed in an upcoming presidential election. Cox acknowledges that Lincoln was an astute politician. Lincoln understood the consequences of alienating an electorate in what was expected to be a close election, but he notes Lincoln responded with a determined sense of justice. True, some Indians had committed serious crimes, yet most of those charged had only been guilty of being on the battlefield, and many had been given assurances that they would be given amnesty if they surrendered. Without adequate counsel, the captives were helpless. Cox praises Lincoln for his compassion and determination to save those whose fate appeared certain -- death by hanging. Of the 303 on death row, Lincoln managed to save all but thirty-eight. Then he ordered that the remaining condemned prisoners should not be "subject to any unlawful violence".

In our present age of political correctness, one might fault Cox for his repeated use of the word "squaw" in place of Indian women, a word that some find offensive. His treatment of the Indian grievances and their plight before the conflict is clearly sympathetic to the natives. He uses the word "Indian" instead of Native Americans, as do most professional historians, and most Indians themselves. The author will be criticized for what appears as gratuitous citing of heinous crimes committed by the undisciplined Indians, especially for the alleged gang rape of young white girls ages twelve and thirteen and for the nailing of children to trees. He justifies including gory details as necessary to help the readers understand the extent of vindictiveness manifested by white Minnesotans after the warfare. He records that after the conflict, locals in Henderson fell upon the Indians with clubs, knives and stones as they were being led to Fort Snelling, and that in New Ulm angry women armed with rocks, pitchforks, bricks and tubs of scalding water to threaten Indians being transferred to the Mankato area. Professional historians are usually more cautious about the use of atrocity accounts when they are derived from hearsay, inflated rumors, or recounted by a later generation and therefore subject to embellishment.

Although Hank H. Cox does not have a list of academic credentials, he appears to have done his basic homework. His overall knowledge of the military, economic and political aspects of the Civil War period is impressive. However, in his ambitious attempt to provide the overall historical setting, one may be detracted from the subject of Lincoln and the Sioux Uprising. The book is eminently readable, but the author's failure to use footnotes is unfortunate. In the biographical notes, the author acknowledges his debt to the Lincoln scholar David Donald and Civil War guru James McPherson. The bibliography includes a number of helpful sources from the Sioux Uprising of 1862.

The book is available in paperback from both Barnes & Noble Booksellers and Amazon.com.

CHAPTER THREE

EDUCATION

EVERYONE IS A WINNER! OR ARE THEY? THE CONSEQUENCES OF GRADE INFLATION

Originally published in *The Lutheran Educator*, number 2, volume 49, December, 2008

The Number of Valedictorians

If all students in a school receive high grades, the school administrator looks good in the community, the teachers are happy they can hand out good news, the students feel amply rewarded for their class attendance and the doting parents are assured all is well. All the way around, every one appears to be a winner. Many schools apparently have that "heavenly" situation. In Seattle, Washington, the 406-member graduating class of 2005 at Garfield High School featured 44 valedictorians with perfect 4.0 grade-point averages. Each of them in over seven semesters never earned less than an A. Last year Garfield had 30 valedictorians, the year before, 27. And nationally, Garfield may be just mid-range. Bullard High School in Fresno, California, graduated 58 valedictorians in 2005. Traditionally the highest-performing student, the valedictorian, gives the final address at graduation; but the increasing number of straight-A students has led some schools to abandon the award altogether ("One High School – 44 Valedictorians," Seattle Times, June 13, 2005, seattletimes.nwsource.com). Even in Minnesota, we too have a preponderance of valedictorians. Minnesota's Eden Prairie High School selected 24 valedictorians in 2007 based on students with a 4.0 GPA. More than 800 high school valedictorians applied to the University of Notre Dame in 2005. That sounds impressive — until you consider that Notre Dame rejected 300 of them. The end is still not in sight. One recent valedictorian surmised: "If there isn't a serious review of valedictorian benchmarks, as the number of valedictorians increases every year, perhaps in a couple of years, there will be more valedictorians than not or even half and half, which might seem ridiculous now but is entirely possible" (Amanda Mene, feature editor of The Paper at Dana Hills High School. This opinion piece was first published in the Feb. 29, 2008, edition of The Paper, myochigh.com).

Grade Inflation Began in the Colleges

If most students in a class receive an A, then they must all be excellent students, or there is a problem known as grade inflation. This inflation is evident in all levels in the academic world, especially at colleges and universities since the 1960s. This has been well documented by studies such as that conducted by Duke professor Stuart Rojstaczer, related in National Trends in Grade Inflation (www.gradeinflation.com). Although the trend is universal, his statistics show private schools undergoing grade inflation at a rate that is about 25-30% higher than public schools.

Those who defend the "feel good" element in charitable grade handouts may shrug this off as a matter of pedagogical value of learning over grading. This is a fuzzy way of saying that the colleges are still turning out better students. Rojstaczer says, such assertions "are of dubious worth." He conjectures that the resurgence of grade inflation in the 1980s principally was caused by the emergence of a consumer-based culture in higher education. Students are paying more for a product every year, and increasingly they want and get the reward of a good grade for their purchase. In this culture, professors are not only compelled to grade more easily, but also to water down course content. Consequently, both intellectual rigor and grading standards have weakened. Another theory is proposed by William Cole: "Perhaps it is not surprising that grade inflation seems to have coincided with the 'opening up' of the curriculum that began in the late 1960's." Cole continues: "Many academics now seem to believe that all cultures, books and fields of study are, in some vague sense, equally valid and thus, in, an even vaguer sense, equally 'good.' (Sound like post-modernism?) Having embraced this relativism, some faculty members may feel that it is incomparable with making absolute judgments of our students. Giving everyone a good grade becomes the path of least resistance" (William Cole, The Chronicle of Higher Education, quoted in *Stanford Review*, vol. XXVII, Issue 7, stanford review.org). There are other theories. An interesting and thoughtful causation list was submitted in an article by Jennifer Franklin and Michael Theal, "My Fight Against Grade Inflation: A Response to William Cole," (Minnesota State University, Mankato, mnsu.edu/cetl/teachingresources). One might also consider evaluation systems in which students grade professors, thereby providing an incentive for teachers to go easy on their future evaluators (Ivy League Grade Inflation, www.usatoday.com/news/opinion/2002/02/08/edtwof2.htm).

Professor Harvey C. Mansfield of Harvard, however, maintains: " Professors who give easy grades gain just a fleeting popularity, salted with disdain. In later life, students will forget those professors; they will remember the ones who posed a challenge" (Harvey Mansfield, "Grade Inflation: It's Time to Face the Facts," *The Chronicle of Higher Education*, chronicle.com/free/v47/i30/30b02401.htm).

There have been some attempts to deal with this malady of grade inflation in colleges. In 1992, at Harvard, 91% of all undergraduate grades were B- or higher. In 1993, 83.6 % of all Harvard seniors graduated with honors. Leaders from a number of institutions, including Harvard University and Princeton University, have publicly stated that grades have been rising. Efforts are being made to change grading practices. If schools can return to using the full range of grades (Stanford University once dropped D's and F's, but then reinstated them), they can better provide a full accounting to students on how they are doing. UC Berkeley has a reputation for rigorous grading policies in some science and engineering classes. Departmental guidelines state that no more than 17% of the students in any given class may be awarded A grades, and that the class GPA should be in the range of 2.7 to 2.9 out of a maximum of 4.0 grade points. Other departments, however, are not adhering to such strict guidelines, as data from the University's Office of Student Research indicates that the average overall undergraduate GPA is about 3.25 (UC Berkeley Undergraduate Fact Sheet – Fall 2004, en.wikipedia.org/wiki/Grade_inflation).

However, since grade inflation is not uniform between schools, students in more stringently graded schools and departments are at an inequitable disadvantage. One hates to admit it, but a C is a killer on a transcript, especially given that an A, in today's society, does not mean "excellent." It wasn't always that way. In a commencement speech delivered to UC Berkeley, Ted Koppel admitted: "I blossomed at Stanford, but I was a C plus student as an undergraduate. As was George W. Bush when he went to Yale." Koppel told the graduating class: "Frankly, given the state of grade inflation these days, it's difficult to argue that the document (diploma) has much value to begin with" (ABC newscaster Ted Koppel's prepared remarks, delivered to UC Berkeley graduates at Commencement Convocation 2004, UC Berkeley News, berkeley.edu/news/media/releases/ 2004/05/14).

SPEAKING OUT

Grade Inflation at the Middle and High School Level

Young students should be taught that grades are not a source of self-esteem, but simply indicate a relative mastery of skills and facts. Grade inflation hinders a true assessment. A study on high school inflation was conducted as an ACT research project in March of 2004. The results support the conclusion that the increase in HSGPA between 1991 and 2003 is due to grade inflation, rather than to an increase in the average level of achievement (David J. Woodruff and Robert L. Ziomek, "High School Grade Inflation," ACT Research Report Series, 2004-4, ww.act.org/research/researchers/ reports).

College Board officials say that the number of college-bound high school students with A averages grew from 28 percent of the total to 38 percent in 10 years -- but their scores fell an average of 12 points on the verbal portion of the SAT and three points on math (William H. Honan, "S.A.T. Scores Decline Even as Grades Rise," *New York Times*, September 2, 1998). To further delve into the question of whether schools that give generous grades to student accomplish more than those who do not, let's look into another study. In 1987, two researchers (Donald Thomas, Ph.D. President Emeritus, School Management Study Group William Bainbridge, Ph.D. President, School Match Corporation, Columbus, Ohio) began to conduct "School Effectiveness Audits to answer a basic question often asked by Boards of Education: "How effective are our schools?" After comprehensive auditing they concluded: "One of the greatest frauds perpetrated on high school students is grade inflation. In general, the highest academic grade inflation is in the lowest achieving schools. Schools which expect little and provide high grades, regardless of the level of academic achievement, are fraudulent educational systems and should be corrected" ("Grade Inflation: The Current Fraud" by M. Donald Thomas, Ph.D. and William Bainbridge, Ph.D., www.endgradeinflation.org).

The inflation problem is also of concern at the middle school level.

Rochester, Minnesota, school district officials had to decide which middle-schoolers would participate in a four-week remedial summer program. Should a high grade point average make students exempt from suggestions that they attend remedial classes? At least one Rochester parent is upset that her 11-year-old son, whom she says earned straight A's, was asked to go to summer school. The school was on the spot. Still, the district would be remiss if the welfare of the student is not foremost. In spite of high grades, that student needed the extra assistance. ("Editorial: Summer School Raises Grade-inflation Issue," *Rochester Post-Bulletin,* June 6, 2008).

Grade Inflation at the Elementary School Level

Grading standards in primary education have received remarkably less attention, though here too, there are problems. According to Maurice E. Lucas and David N. Figlio there are two major questions related to grading standards in the elementary school. First, to what degree do the grades distributed by schools and teachers correspond to their students' performance on state and national exams? Second, and more important, how does "tough" or "easy" grading affects students' learning? The data used consisted of observations on almost every 3rd, 4th and 5th grader in the school system of Gainesville, Florida, between the 1995–96 and 1998–99 school years. Standardized measurements provided a unique advantage for a study of this nature because it administers the Iowa Test of Basic Skills (ITBS), a nationally normed exam, and the Florida Comprehensive Assessment Test (FCAT).

The researchers found that these Florida teachers varied considerably in their grading standards, even within a single school district. In fact, the teachers' grading standards often varied as much within a single school as within the school district as a whole. Overall, their results suggest that elementary-school students (both high and low level achievers) learn more with "tough" teachers. Variance depended on students' individual performance levels and on the overall performance level of their classrooms. The study also revealed that the teachers who are tough graders are significantly more likely to hold Master's degrees. The advantage of holding higher standards is that the students are then devoted to working harder. In the case of weaker students, there is also the possibility that their parents may devote more attention to helping with schoolwork when grades suggest that there is such a need (David N. Figlio, professor of economics at the University of Florida and a research associate of the National Bureau of Economic Research and Maurice E. Lucas director of research and assessment for the school board of Alachua County, Florida, "The Gentleman's A, "Hoover Institution, www.Hover.org).

Should all students in the class be successful? Yes, in that each individual achieve at an appropriate level for him or herself, but not everyone should receive the blue ribbon grade of excellence. Everyone has value, but not everyone has the same talent or work ethic. If we award credit for a level of performance, then that level should have been achieved. In our present self-esteem society, we want everyone to succeed and receive the highest awards, even if it rewards mediocre work. That is like giving a large number of 4H participants a blue ribbon at a state fair. The rationale behind group awards, or the Danish method used by some 4H organizations, is that it allegedly "provides recognition for the maximum number of 4-H members... in recognition of a basic need of all young people and that public recognition for achievement helps fulfill this basic need" (Danish or Group Method of Judging, 4h.wsu.edu/projects/danishsys.htm). One club newsletter to children advertised: "In most 4-H shows and classes, everyone can get a blue award"(Award Ribbons, www.4h.uiuc.edu/staff/newkids/letter4.pdf). A participation ribbon might be in order, but is the highest award meaningful if they are distributed to most of the entrants? This observation is not meant to belittle the fine 4H program, which is of tremendous benefit to young people, but to illustrate the prevalence of award inflation.

EDUCATION

Real Competition for Grades Is Healthy

Those who favor easy rewards may have good intentions, such as reducing tension and stress. Yet, we could submit that healthy competition is good, and that a degree of stress is beneficial. Professor Mansfield of Harvard has maintained: "Grade inflation has resulted from the emphasis in American education on the notion of self-esteem. According to that therapeutic notion, the purpose of education is to make students feel capable and empowered. So to grade them, or to grade them strictly, is cruel and dehumanizing. Grading creates stress. It encourages competition rather than harmony. It is judgmental."(Harvey Mansfield, "Grade Inflation: It's Time to Face the Facts." *The Chronicle of Higher Education*, April 6, 2001). Is upfront honest evaluation helpful or harmful?

True, stress over grades can have unsettling consequences. Some youngsters may experience headaches, stomach pain and test time jitters. Yet, stress has an upside. Concern about grades and performance releases adrenaline and other hormones that improve performance. More blood flows to the brain and enhances our ability to do our best. "Your goal shouldn't be to get rid of stress," contends Esther Sternberg, a researcher at the National Institute of Health and author of *The Balance Within: The Science Connecting Health and Emotions.* Rather, she says, "You should aim for the appropriate stress response" (Deborah Kotz, "Relax! Stress, if Managed, Can Be Good for You," *U.S. News & World Report*, June 16, 2008). Stress response should be appropriate for individual situations. Students need to learn to accept and control stress and this begins with attitude, learning to confront challenges (coping strategies) and having realistic expectations (Stress of Students: Healthful stress management strategies,www.uark.edu/~caps/Stress). Having survived, even thrived, in college yourself, you might have useful insights or tips to offer your students. I personally found that as a DMLC student, if I studied more and worked harder, my comfort level before major tests was greater because I felt more confident. Keeping up on class assignments and periodically reviewing notes to avoid last minute cramming had the same effect. These strategies not only help reduce the stress and improve the grades, they make education a learning experience. Real achievement brings about real self-esteem.

Competition helps bring out the best in our students. Witness the benefits of spelling bees, debate teams, science fairs, track meets, athletic team competitions, band chair positions, making the choir… We encourage Christians to make the best of their God given abilities and to develop disciplined skills in various areas of proficiency so that they might better serve the Lord throughout their lives.

There is a danger of being under-stressed all the time so that a person cannot cope when a real crisis occurs in the outside world. A lack of challenge induces boredom and ultimately low energy and a lack of self-esteem, which ironically, is what some modern educators hope to alleviate by inflated grading and reduced test taking.

Prepare Students for the Real World

Once graduates enter the job market, they may discover fierce competition. Students entering the marketplace will find not only competition for jobs, but also for wages, for advancement within the workplace and for business. There can be consequences of being too laid back. Applications for drivers' licenses may be turned down and tests required to be retaken. Poor production may mean the loss of a job. Complacent or careless handling of a business in a competitive market could lead to profit losses or bankruptcy. We do not live in a purely socialistic society where we can complacently expect the government to solve all our problems in spite of our weaknesses. A classroom without personal accountability for performance fosters mediocrity the same way. Some students will not work very hard if they know their chance of getting an A anyway is good, or at least they can count on mustering a soft B. In that milieu, gifted students can just cruise along without effort for the easy A or soft B. No wonder so many high school and college students work just about full time. Does grade inflation motivate students to do their very best and become academic achievers? An article in *The Chronicle of Higher Education* states, "Nineteen percent of full-time freshman in college say they spend only 1 to 5 hours per week preparing for classes. Seniors who answered the same survey reported studying even less than freshman…" ("The Initiative to End Grade Inflation," endgradeinflation.org). That is a very sad situation!

Rewarding the truly studious and the exceptional student increases output. The Synod Ad Hoc Committee recommended to the District Conventions in 2008 "that we foster excellence by encouraging an environment where a significant percentage of each class at Martin Luther College is vying for scholarships tied to academic merit, reminding students that grades matter." The rationale given is that "this would encourage competition" as students strive for the rewards (Ad Hoc Commission, Preliminary Report and Recommendations, 2008, wels.net). This same approach is advocated for recruitment purposes at our Lutheran high schools so that we garner the best students for entrance to Martin Luther College. In the end the Kingdom work of the church benefits from this approach.

Integrity and Reporting Honestly

Is inflation of grades a matter of dishonesty? To a degree it is, even if everyone seems to be doing it. Jay A. Halfond, Dean of Boston University's Metropolitan College, contends: "Grading is about fundamental fairness. Not everyone performs exceptionally well and should not be deceived into thinking they have. Nobody's achievements should be cheapened by a leveling of grades" (Jay A. Halfond, "Grade Inflation Is Not A Victimless Crime," *Christian Science Monitor,* csmonitor.com).

Social promotion might well be considered as avoiding responsibility. Giving passing grades when passing grades are not really reflective of a child's ability to do the work is unconscionable. Promoting those who lack the skills of the standards required for moving to more difficult material merely shunts them off to a more a difficult situation later on. Pat Vallas, CEO of the Chicago Public Schools, maintains: "When you socially promote, you not only hurt the children who are not meeting minimum standards by promoting them to another grade level where they really can't do the work, but you are also hurting the children who are at grade level or above, because you are basically putting those children in a classroom where the teacher is forced to lower his or her standards. So the net effect is the child who is behind never gets caught up, and the child who is at grade level or above suffers." Chicago made some changes. Summer school is now mandatory for third, sixth, eighth and ninth graders, who scored two years below grade level on national norm tests ("Social Promotion," Online Newshour www.pbs.org/newshour/bb/education/ jan-june99/retention). Chicago Mayor Richard M. Daley criticized teachers who adhered to the philosophy "just get 'em ahead, who cares, get 'em in high school, maybe they'll drop out; get 'em out of the system." He stated flatly: "No more social promotions" in Chicago schools. ("Higher Learning," Online Newshour, www.pbs.org/newshour/bb/education/ july-dec97/schools). In the long run, students will be better served and most parents will appreciate the upfront honesty of such a policy.

What about students with learning disabilities (LD)? Most schools, if not all schools, use the accommodation/modification approach. Government requirements have set forth an inclusion model and since July 1, 1998, students with disabilities are to be included in statewide assessments which create a general presumption that students with disabilities will not only "participate" in the general curriculum to the maximum extent possible, but will also be held to standards of accountability. All children, including children with disabilities, must demonstrate mastery in a given area of the general curriculum before allowing them to progress to the next level or grade in that area. That means the teacher may make appropriate changes to help these children learn, but may not fundamentally alter or lower the standard or expectation of the course, standard or test (Dean B. Eggert, "Grading Students with Educational Disabilities," http://www.bridges4kids.org).

To this end Special Education teachers are added to faculties to make accommodations and modifications for LD students. Those thus trained devise effective teaching strategies that will help LD students be successful in a regular classroom. These teachers adjust by using alternative teaching strategies, which accommodates the different kinds of intelligences and learning styles. Annette Wulff, a Special Education teacher who taught a number of years in the New Ulm public schools at the secondary level, has seen a number of her "disabled" students respond so successfully to modified strategies that they are then able to go to go on and do well in college, some even achieving a place on the honor roll (Annette Wulff, awulff@newulmtel.net). Otherwise, those "failing students," who are just moved along, never reach their full potential. What a difference in the lives of these students because their disabilities were not covered over with soft grades and/or social promotion!

Look in the Mirror

No doubt the vast majority of the WELS "everyday" teachers try to be fair-minded, are dedicated and committed to doing the best they can for each of their students. Anyone familiar with WELS teachers from kindergarten through our college and seminary can attest to their character and sincere devotion to their calling. Yet, it behooves us to review the nationwide problem of grade inflation that seems to entrap us in the web as well. The grade inflation phenomenon has flooded the country and we also are challenged to make adjustments as necessary. A few in the public area have come forth to meet the challenge of grade inflation. University of Colorado president Hank Brown wanted to take on grade inflation by disclosing class rank or grade-point-average percentiles on student transcripts. Brown proposed to regents that the university change transcripts to give potential employers or graduate schools a clearer picture of student achievement ("Brown Assails Grade

Inflation," *Denver Post*, 08/31/2006). The average class grade listed on the transcript would make the report more meaningful. Standardized tests, whatever their flaws might be, are an increasingly crucial tool in determining academic abilities ("Editorial: Summer School Raises Grade-inflation Issue," *Rochester Post-Bulletin*, June 6, 2008).

The Remedy

Actually, any kind of diagnostic information besides grades would be helpful to parents with children in elementary and high schools. The inability to commit to an "honest" grading policy reduces the efficiency of making level assignments for students who transfer or graduate. Deception even though well intended, causes confusion. Students who do not perform up to basic levels should be so informed. It's like saving a drowning kid. The sooner you get to him the better. Teachers who give most students A's and B's only defeat the purpose of grades to motivate students to improve and work up to their abilities or to help parents and employers to distinguish actual abilities and achievement. If kids are in danger of falling short, they and their parents shouldn't be led down a primrose path with inflated report cards. And if students and/or parents challenge teachers, administrators need to back up teachers who give out realistic grades.

Everyone wants to be liked, and our Christian teachers are no exception. It can be all too easy to succumb to pressure to dole out high grades. Such pressure may come from diplomatic administrators, easy going faculty members, assertive parents or outspoken students, but our responsibility as professional Christian teachers must be paramount. From top to bottom, we need to put our standards of actual grades of achievement first. Our students may be great kids, even winners, but they can't all be valedictorians.

EDUCATION

RESPONSE TO EVERYONE IS A WINNER... GRADE INFLATION

E-mail letter from the Editor of the Northwestern Publishing House

Professor Wulff,

A note to thank you for your article and insights on grade inflation. I hope all our teachers read and take it to heart. In our society it must be a real struggle for young teachers to put your words into practice.

Lord's blessings,

Bob Koester

Editor, NPH

PUBLIC SCHOOL TEACHERS NEED SENORITY RIGHTS

Published as a Letter to the Editor, New Ulm Journal

We Should Retain the Experienced Teachers

We read so much in the *Minneapolis Star Tribune* how "progress" has been made in the move towards eliminating seniority rights of teachers in public education. Some have argued that this makes it easier to remove unqualified teachers, but a blanket policy of terminating seniority rights comes with a terrible price. Cash strapped school systems could feel compelled to release good faithful experienced teachers because they are the best paid. In these bleak economic times, cutting veteran teachers may seem to provide an easy fix for balancing the budget. Students should have the best teachers, not the cheapest.

Respect for Service

Another major concern I have is for teachers who are cut loose after putting in their best years for a school district. It could be tough for older teachers to find employment elsewhere and possibly face hardships moving to another location. How easy would it be to terminate a person just short of retirement age and leave them in the lurch? How easy would it be for a control person to fire a veteran teacher for petty reasons or even religious beliefs? If a teacher should be incompetent, that person should have been denied tenure in the beginning, or else removed when deficiencies first became evident. Younger people can more readily retrain and find employment elsewhere. Many bad teachers seek employment elsewhere on their own anyway to something more fitting to their disposition. Teaching is demanding work. The fact that any teacher has staying power is somewhat evidence of dedication and acceptable performance.

Making Exceptions

Of course, if true incompetence crops up, it should not be tolerated by the administration or defended by the union. Also, it does make some sense to limiting seniority rights within a given discipline. A school district should not be required to transfer a veteran teacher to a position for which they have not been trained. In general, however, seniority rights make sense.

Attracting Future Teachers

How can we attract future teachers to public education if they can be so easily discarded arbitrarily or easily removed in favor of younger and less expensive replacements? Hopefully the legislators in St. Paul move cautiously on this seniority issue.

Frederick Wulff, New Ulm

EDUCATION

THE TEACHER AS MORE THAN A FACILITATOR

Originally published in The Lutheran Educator

Teachers and principals often serve as facilitators. A facilitator is someone who skillfully helps a group of people understand their common objectives and assists them in planning to achieve them without taking a particular position in the discussion. He/she utilizes the talent of the group in a democratic manner that best serves the interest of the school. The role has been likened to that of a midwife who assists in the process but is not the producer of the end result. An effective principal or administrator is by necessity a good facilitator. Can the same application of the term apply to classroom instruction of children?

The Facilitator of Substance

When I was doing course work in diplomatic history at the University of Wisconsin, I once had a guest instructor from Purdue University. The students in the class were rather lethargic to his lecture approach so he shifted to an interactive mode and tried to present himself more as a facilitator. At first I thought this great because I liked to interact with my professors. However, to my disappointment, the class hour became more of a bull session where my classmates contributed animated exchanges of nonsense. They had no real knowledge of history or any kind of background to recognize the difference between fuzzy feelings and the real world. Frankly, we were wasting time. I was thankful when the professor went back to the "old hat lecture" whereby he shared his depth in his specialized subject area.

At the risk of being branded old fashioned I offer the advice that sometimes our teachers should be more than facilitators. True, lectures can be boring and class interaction is extremely important, but surely there is a middle ground. Teaching which is primarily facilitating is likely to have pitfalls. Students, even college students, sometimes lack background substance. Modern educators like to shy away from stress on building content background, or on teachers as authority figures, but class activities should be based on more than shallow assumptions or personal viewpoints.

The Facilitator and Neutrality

One of the problems encountered with the teacher-as-facilitator procedure is that he or she is supposed to be a "content neutral party" -- one who does not take sides or express a point of view during the discussion and one who promotes mutual understanding. A teacher may draw on the knowledge of the members of the class or on what the individuals gleaned from the society around them. Like brainstorming, this has value, but it should only be the starting point. All contributions should be considered, but not all contributions are of equal value. This delineation must be stressed. In the area of history, for example, students may be led to believe that there are no real answers, only differing viewpoints. True, finding "truth" in history is a very complex challenge because of the subjectivity factor, but there are guidelines for prioritizing different kinds of information. There is a difference between discernable fact and speculation, between honest enquiry and propaganda, between the works of recognized scholars and shallow chatter on talk shows (or by movie stars), and in the case of Biblical history between absolute truth and faulty reason. The sources of information and levels of reliability should always be stressed in class discussions.

The Facilitator and Curriculum Standards

The school board, administration and faculty should have authority over the history curriculum; anything short of this control is shortsighted. A democratic, student-centered approach, in which the teacher is only a facilitator to suggest topics, is an abrogation of responsibility. An analogy might be that parents must do more than suggest what food their children eat if they want them to have a healthy nutritious diet. Sometimes well-meaning teachers try to promote learner autonomy and responsibility for the learning process, but the students really are not mature enough or wise enough to know what is best for them. Doesn't human nature tend to take the easier road rather than that which is of most benefit? Would children understand the importance of constitutional history over against popular or romantic cultural topics? Is it wise to create huge gaps in their understanding of the continuity in history or allow happenstance to prevail over sequential learning? Do we want some periods of history repeated at the expense of other? Can children make wise choices if they are not acquainted with the broader subject? We may not want children to cover history only for content's sake, but surely there must be some overall plan. Meaningful content needs to be the focus and offered through vigorous interaction and thoughtful discussion.

The Facilitator and Post Modernism

Let's admit it. Post Modernism has pervaded modern educational philosophical thought throughout our nation's educational systems. We always like to think of this trend as something associated with others, but we might well ask if some of this philosophy hasn't also moved into the ranks of Christian education? In a recent article of *The Lutheran Educator*, Dr. Jim Norwine released findings from his study on this topic, reporting that 39% of students in parochial or church affiliated colleges believe "everybody's point of view is equally valid" (Dr. Jim Norwine, "Are Our Students' Values Postmodern" *The Lutheran Educator*, May, 2007). Our society is rapidly changing. We are living in an age of "the new tolerance" that teaches we must tolerate everything --- except upholding traditional values. Recent graduates from a prominent Lutheran College here in Minnesota, who were living together as an unmarried couple, explained to me in a casual manner, our parents have their sub-cultural values and we have our sub-cultural values. Why should they question what we do? An interesting and thought provoking book on this subject is *The New Tolerance* by Josh McDowell and Bob Hostetler (Wheaton, Illinois, 1998). This book may be worth consideration for the school or church library.

The Post Modernist believes that each person constructs his or her own reality. This attitude encourages a belief in relativism and subsequently results in a collapse of morality. "One view is as good as another" is espoused, and right and wrong are considered a matter of individual opinion. The break-up of the family, increased divorce rates, prevalence of non-married parents and other social maladies result. Facilitators naturally promote tolerance towards the views of others, encourage mutual understanding and foster the search for inclusive solutions. These could be very noble goals. We need to be careful about making tolerance an end in itself. A few years ago I wrote a lengthy article on the need to appreciate and cherish other cultures (Frederick Wulff, "Build Bridges to Other Cultures," *The Lutheran Educator*, February, 2004). No doubt we should promote tolerance and acceptance of others. Scripture tells us "to do to others as you would have them do to you"(Luke 6:31). But tolerance should not mean respecting or embracing false teachings and sinful behavior.

The Facilitator and Judgmentalism

Dr. Norwine warns of " a growing extreme toleration whereby judgmentalism is made a social sin." He cited one of his students who believed that while the honor killings of Muslim women by their own family members were terrible, the student felt she had no right to impose her own values on a person of another culture" (Norwine, *TLE*, May, 2007). When we as teachers of history present unsavory practices like the horrors of the Holocaust, we can and should say that this brutal killing of millions of people is wrong. The suicide bombers who murder innocent families in the market place are not to be excused as freedom fighters or liberators. Honest judgments are warranted. If we sanitize our teaching to avoid judgment, we cover our heads in the sand of the new tolerance.

Yet, this does not mean that we want to be clothed in obnoxious negativity that harshly condemns anything we do not agree with, or as unloving people who are quick to make uncharitable judgments. A Christian strives to live at peace with all men (Romans 12:18). Jesus enunciated "You have heard that it was said, 'Love your neighbor and hate your enemy.' But I tell you: Love your enemies and pray for those who persecute you, that you may be sons of your Father in heaven. He causes his sun to rise on the evil and the good, and sends rain on the righteous and the unrighteous. If you love those who love you, what reward will you get? Are not even the tax collectors doing that? And if you greet only your brothers, what are you doing more than others? Do not even pagans do that? (Matthew 5: 43-47). We do not hate others or wish harm to those who disagree with our Christian principles. Christians share a commonality with those outside the faith. We are all sinners and all people are sought out by Jesus to come to the knowledge of truth. Our relationship with others, even those whose beliefs and behaviors seem reprehensible, should be one of kindness and love. We especially need to share the clear teaching of Scripture and pray that God the Holy Spirit will bring them to know that Jesus is the only way to eternal life (John 14:6). It will not be easy. Jesus said: "The world... hates me because I testify that what it does is evil"(John 7:7).

Pluralism, which insists all opinions have the same value, sounds wonderful to the modern educator and the tolerance-obsessed minds, but it is flawed thinking. The entertainment industry spreads post modernist "understanding" and "anything goes" fuzziness (to foster self esteem) into the homes of those we teach. Talk show hosts often make traditional Christians out to be bigots because Christians interpret Scripture literally. In the face of "the new tolerance" (actually intolerance) we should not waver.

It is tempting to strive to be in the forefront of educational methodology along with leaders in public education, but caution is in order. It takes wisdom to recognize the pitfalls in some of these new trends and guts to stand up to them. True, facilitators can be effective teachers, but the insidious spread of postmodernism and the "new tolerance" is cause for concern. We simply must be more than facilitators in our classroom. Above all we need to teach with the responsibility that God has given us through our calls as Christian teachers.

INSENSITIVE TEACHERS

Letter to the Editor of Preach the Gospel (submitted but was not published; the editor replied by phone)

To Managing Editor:

I have just received my *Preach the Gospel* magazine in the mail and want to thank you for this excellent publication. I enjoyed it from the attractive cover to the closing statement by President Wendland. Very professional. The articles were well written and the many photos helped make your ministry live. However, I thought there was one downside. A quote of (name withheld) about his vicarage training could give the impression that his "bishop" made fun of weaker students (laugh, laugh) when he evaluated their submitted sermons. (Name withheld) may have been encouraged by this "rough handling" as he calls it, but there are others who might have been better served by encouragement (as Peter Unnasch mentioned in another article). We have all probably had a bad teacher, like the bishop, but this quotation by (name withheld) could give the impression that this is the norm. I wish the editor had caught that because surely this is not the case. Otherwise the magazine is commendable and should be shared by others. We have much to be thankful for in our seminary and its vital service in Kingdom work. Keep up the good work. In his name, Frederick Wulff (retired MLC professor)

EDUCATION

RESPONSE TO INSENSITIVE TEACHER

NOTE: The managing editor called me on the phone. He apologized for not catching that. He assured me that the professor cited in the article is a very kind person and that the particular characterization of him is not representative of his teaching.

BOOK REVIEW

Book Review of *Teaching With Documents: Using Primary Sources from the National Archives and Records Administration*, Washington, D.C. National Council for the Social Studies in The Lutheran Educator, volume 32, number 3, February, 1992

This book resulted from a collaboration of the National Archives and the National Council for the Social Studies. The end product was a spiral bound book containing fifty-two source documents—maps, letters, memoirs, drawings, and photographs— that will help teachers guide children into the past. History becomes real for the students as they learn to look at the evidence left by the participants. Students can read brief eyewitness accounts, usually one page in length, from significant moments of our nation's history. This provides opportunities for them to realize that a study of documents requires interpretation and recognition of bias and subjectivity. It is hoped that students will then employ these evaluation skills as they confront information in daily newspapers and television programs.

This book was made for teachers. Every document is preceded by introductory historical information. The documents, photographed reproductions of the originals, are usually full page in size and easy to duplicate for handouts to the students. The documents are followed by a number of helpful teaching suggestions and activities for the classroom. The preface to the book also offers suggestions to teachers on how they might locate and assemble documents on their own. The book offers a wide variety of interesting and worthwhile documents. There are a number that could enhance history classes. This book is worth investigating as a useful social studies tool for grades eight through twelve.

Frederick Wulff

CHAPTER FOUR
RELIGION AND CHRISTIAN LIFE

INITIATING THE NEW KID

> Originally submitted to *The Lutheran Educator*, but the editors felt constrained not to publish it. I expected that decision because the topic is controversial in our circles.

Initiation, or Is It Hazing?

We have all, at one time or another, been the new kid on the block, the incoming freshman at school, or a fresh recruit in some club or organization. More than likely we were initiated in some way. In an unfamiliar setting, being a rookie can be an unsettling experience – sometimes scary. How are newcomers treated at your school or an organization of which you are responsible? Is the experience of the new kid a pleasant one or is it an ordeal?

To initiate means to begin, coming from the Latin *initium*. It starts with the newcomer who is striving to become one of the group. In our WELS schools, this beginning also has been accompanied by initiations. Can the term initiation be equated with the harsher sounding word "hazing"? Will Kelm, PhD, in his book *The Power of Caring*, says, "If you have to ask if it's hazing, it is. "According to Elizabeth J. Allan, Ph.D. University of Maine, "Hazing is defined in terms of the following core components: 1) Hazing involves behavior that is humiliating, degrading, emotionally and/or physically harmful. 2) Hazing is behavior that is expected in order to join or maintain one's full status in a group or membership organization. 3) Hazing can occur regardless of an individual's willingness to participate." Is this something that is compatible with our Christian philosophy when we are bringing someone into a close-knit organization?

Frequent misconceptions about hazing include the idea that it is nothing more than harmless pranks, a practice largely isolated to college fraternities. The reality is that hazing activities occur in many different arenas such as a summer camp, a sports team, a youth organization, middle school, high school, college or even a vocation. ("Myths and Facts about Hazing" www.StopHazing.com).

The Old School of Thought

Hazing goes a long way back and was prevalent in Reformation Germany. According to cultural historian Michael Olmert, 16th century initiations were thought "to test the mettle of the candidates and to temper a novice against the buffets that life would send." Inculcating a sense of humility was part of the mix. Luther was a product of the time and even officiated at a hazing of new Wittenberg students in July of 1539, telling his charges to be patient with the ritual since they would face various vexations later in life (Michael Olmert, "Points of Origin," *Smithsonian*, September, 1983, pp.150-154).

Unfortunately, this tradition of initiating or hazing new students continued and was even widely used in the recent past among Synod ministerial training personnel. Still, these sincere and dedicated church workers have taught and preached God's Word and future generations in the Synod will be grateful for their service -- and honor them in same sense that we honor Luther. With due respect to the old school, the old attitudes toward initiations stemmed from flawed cultural presuppositions. In the more recent past, church school administrators and instructors continued sanctioning initiations with the perception that they were a good preparation or seasoning process for students. Justification given for this practice in WELS was threefold: it toughened students for the ministry, it created a bonding among the student body and it taught freshmen humility (documentation upon request, *fredwulff@newulmtel.net*).

First of all, the proposition that "it toughened kids up for a life in the ministry" is faulty. Possibly there was a cultural link that perceived meekness, sympathy and emotions as weaknesses, and we should be tough. The time-honored initiations could be heartless and take on the appearance of being mean spirited. The unintended consequence encouraged students to subdue feelings for those in a distressful situation and thus numb their sensitivity. Writer Hank Nuwer, a well known expert on hazing, aptly puts it: "Hazing is an extraordinary activity that, when it occurs often enough, becomes perversely ordinary as those who engage in it grow desensitized to its inhumanity." (Nuwer's *Wrongs of Passage*, p. 31). Psychologist D'Arcy Lyness, PhD, says, "When people are in a group they often relax individual responsibility, assuming that someone else will act when it's appropriate" (http://kidshealth.org/parent/emotions/behavior/hazing.html).

Eventually activity that normally would be considered out of place took on the appearance of being acceptable and legitimate. Hence, attempts to "toughen up" students for ministry sometimes resulted in unfavorable publicity for the Church (documentation upon request, fredwulff@newulmtel.net). Secondly, initiation was considered by some instructors to have an added benefit because it instilled a bond or loyalty to the institution and student body. The proponents argued that hazing is a way for people to demonstrate their commitment to a group, creating a sense of oneness. On the surface this appears a noble goal. Evidence supports that initiations may bond somewhat, but there are other ways to establish firm lasting relationships without crude behavior. Brad Childress, the no-nonsense football coach of the Minnesota Vikings, prohibited all hazing of rookie players, beginning in 2006, just because he does not want division among his players. This head coach insists the Vikings work together as a team. He feels that an activity like taping new players to a goalpost disrupts harmony among team members. Working together without ill feelings is a better bonding catalyst, not only in sports, but also among organizations in general. Besides, our real bonding agent, or super glue, is the Gospel.

Thirdly, we could well question the proposition that initiation or hazing taught a humility that was good for incoming students. Military boot training manuals used to claim such a transformation, but sociological studies show no real transformation takes place. Recruits simply mask their behavior and do not internalize a new role. Actually, at the college level, it is the upper classmen who wield the controlling hand and are more likely to benefit from a course on humility, if anyone would. Furthermore, those of us who have helped register incoming college students would characterize a newcomer at registration as more like having "hat in hand." Since freshmen at any level of education are in unfamiliar territory, they are likely to approach the new setting with uncertainty and a sense of trepidation.

Opportunities for the Bully

Even those who express what they consider to be positive effects of initiations will have to admit there are practitioners who cross the line during initiations. Proponents of initiations may have absolutely no intention of harming anyone, but there may also be a few bullies who use this occasion as a license to release venom. Some individuals enjoy a "power trip" at the expense of someone else (StopHazing.org 1998-2005). Initiations nationwide all too often have gotten out of hand. The country was shocked recently when a student at Glenbrook North High School (outside of Chicago) videotaped some junior girls being beaten and covered with mud, feces, pig entrails, garbage and paint by a group of seniors. These were girls hurting girls so severely that a number of them had to be hospitalized. This is an extreme example, to be sure, but anyone who has resided in a male dormitory during initiation time can recall some nasty over-the-line abuses.

Emotional Scars

Even if no physical harm is done, initiations can leave lasting negative feelings and/or emotional injuries. Hazing at any age can be exceedingly harmful. Hazing for young teens is particularly troubling because the developmental stages of adolescence create a situation in which many students are more vulnerable to peer pressure due to their tremendous need for belonging, making friends and finding approval in their peer group. What may appear as "only deflating egos" could have a devastating effect, especially on a young kid away from the protecting environment of the home and family for the first time.

Fond Memories or Nightmares?

We all have heard tales of the "good old days" when we were freshmen and of having upper classmen, sometimes dressed in military garb, dish it out. But these tales are often filtered by age, and over time repeated stories play down the hurt and the harsh realities. Some look back upon those humiliations and painful experiences as not so bad after all – even with fond memories. An interesting essay about Forsan Public High School in Texas relates experiences just that way. One freshman recalled being "decorated" with lipstick, having raw eggs smeared on his face (having the mess remain on his face all day), swallowing raw eggs and racing down the "belt line" as seniors did their best to connect with their belts. Yet, the writer came to accept this as "not so bad after all" (Rodney, Hammack: "Essay on Initiations of Forsan Public High School," Forsan, Texas).

Some tough kids may actually remember such things fondly and popular students may not have been meted out a full measure. However, to the "strange" kid who just didn't fit in, the insecure shy person or some boy who seemed to have effeminate ways, the dose often was upped somewhat. Many very gifted students who like to study may have been labeled as nerds. The proud or stubborn could be targeted to break their spirits. Students can be tough on those they deem different. To such vulnerable victims, initiation might be recalled as a "nightmare from hell." Kids who attended schools away from home may have dropped out because they couldn't cope with the ordeal. Administrators could easily attribute such departures to "just homesickness."

Many women who attended our secondary schools in the good old days do have fond memories of their freshmen year. As far as this writer knows, initiations of female students throughout WELS schools, with few exceptions, have not been harsh. For freshmen women, initiation was usually little more than an embarrassment of inconvenience, like missing sleep and/or missing assignment preparations when overzealous sophomores initiated them overtime. I believe most of our lady teachers would find hazing as depicted in other parts of this article very remote from their own experiences. Hopefully this assessment is correct.

Giving Offense

Today the press and television make so much of perceived inappropriate school mascots or logos, as in North Dakota where a college had its athletic affiliation threatened over a Native American symbol. Nationwide publicity was given to remarks made by a Harvard president who said that women might process information differently from men. This resulted in his removal from office. We have to be careful of the image we project to the public. What message could be sent to the community when freshmen are observed being paraded in undignified ways or chanting demeaning phrases? Any public display of hazing that demeans in any way really reflects badly on the entire school. The public, and many of our own laymen expect more from a Christian school, and well they should. Care must be taken that we do not cause offense by what we might consider to be a harmless tradition.

Making Adjustments

Some would say that because the desire to initiate is a very ancient, deep impulse, it should not be suppressed by regulations. According to this argument, it may then become secret and dangerous. However, I submit that Christian teachers using the tool of the Gospel can keep these impulses in check. Demand zero tolerance. If any inclination towards hazing crops up, our love for our mission and our students should motivate us to nip it in the bud. If hazing exists, it is because we permit it to exist. State lawmakers apparently think it can be suppressed because hazing is illegal in most states. This applies to private schools as well. Only Alaska, Montana, South Dakota, Hawaii, New Mexico and Wyoming don't have anti-hazing laws (Robert Kennedy, "Hazing: --Tradition or Illegal Activity," wwwprivateschool.about.com/cs/students/a/hazing). Furthermore, throughout the United States military structure, there are strict policies and serious consequences for hazing activities.

Thankfully, many of our Lutheran schools and organizations have discontinued this outdated tradition. If any vestiges remain, administrators have a responsibility to take the lead to remove them. Those in charge should insist that activities held by clubs or organizations within the school be appraised and monitored. Keep in mind that church organizations and schools are subject to legal action for negligence. We live in a litigious society and church institutions are not immune to costly lawsuits if they overlook or condone inappropriate behavior. Student consent cannot be used as a defense in a civil law suit. According to law, anyone who allows hazing to occur is a "hazing enabler" (www.StopHazing.com). Litigation may be an important factor to consider, but our noble calling to further God's kingdom is an even greater factor. Teachers and administrators must push to establish clear guidelines of what is and what is not acceptable behavior toward those newcomers who desire to become part of the group. The best way to combat the problem of initiations is for instructors to speak out and to encourage students to speak out as well. Change will not take place if we respectfully remain quiet and let go unchallenged the unwritten code of silence about initiations.

No Nonsense Guidelines

School boards, administrators and faculty should give serious consideration to formulating printed guidelines concerning an initiation policy, if their institution does not already have one. There are many models in existence; perhaps you have one to share. Here in Minnesota, two Catholic universities have formulated policies that have merit:

> "Any kind of hazing is strictly forbidden by the College of Saint Benedict and Saint John's University and subject to severe sanction. Hazing is defined as any action taken or situation created by an individual or group, intentionally or unintentionally, whether on or off college or university premises, to produce mental or physical discomfort, embarrassment, harassment, ridicule or in any way demean the dignity of another human being.... Individuals involved with hazing may be expelled from school, suspended from enrollment for a definite or indefinite period of time and/or face additional sanctions " (CSB|SJU The J-Book, College of Saint Benedict | Saint John's University, Copyright 2004, last revised on August 11, 2005).

Assimilating the New Kid with Christian Kindness

The WELS has been richly blessed with gifted students. We have to marvel at the caliber of the Christian students entrusted to our worker training schools year after year. These students give shining testimony to the value of Christian education – manifesting the power of the Word that was brought to them by dedicated parents, teachers and pastors. The Evil One would like nothing better than to get his foot in our social and institutional systems, passing off the "harmless fun" of

RELIGION AND CHRISTIAN LIFE

hazing as having value. Bible study offers the best bulwark of defense and also help for students who encounter difficult times of transition.

The leaders of our schools need to cultivate a spirit of living the Gospel with which we have been so richly blessed. Tell the students their treatment of the new kid in and out of the classroom should be a reflection of a personal living faith. Encourage students to be a mirror of God's love. Enlighten them concerning the new kid's need for Christian friendship, compassion, comfort and help. Convince them that a fellow student can really be a godsend. Develop a peer-mentoring program within your school or organization. We might borrow ideas from the Link Crew concept that connects new students with upper class mentors. About 50 of Minnesota's 341 school districts have become customers of the Boomerang Project based in Santa Cruz, California (www.linkcrew.com). The *Minneapolis Star Tribune* of 9/01/06 refers to these efforts as "triggering a welcome that resembles an initiation in reverse."

Some of our WELS schools have fostered a Big Brother/Big Sister arrangement that cushions the transition for students to a new setting. This can be extremely important for boarding schools where major adjustments must be made in the absence of parents. At Martin Luther College, professors write personal letters to their assigned advisees before they arrive on campus. Packets are mailed out. When the freshmen arrive in New Ulm upperclassmen greet them, unload their cars and move their belongings into the dorms. Interactive programs are planned before classes. These practices for newcomers are worth emulating.

Some anthropologists promote a coming of age concept that stresses the importance of having road marks in our life to indicate a new level of maturity or progress. Well, if we wish to have some initiation event to mark the beginning of becoming a new member of a team, organization, class or student body, we might look to Christian examples of milestone markers. We became children of God through the visible sacrament of Baptism and we became communicants through the rite of Confirmation. When we became called workers of the kingdom, we solemnly gathered together for Call Day in the chapel. As we entered the public ministry, we were installed or ordained in a ceremony. Possibly we could have a special and meaningful event or service to welcome the new kid as he/she reaches the membership status of the group, and the sooner the better. Celebrate the birth of a new relationship – without any labor pains.

Frederick Wulff is a retired professor of MLC and resides in New Ulm, MN. Comments may be directed to fredwulff@newulmtel.net

---

Detailed accounts of high school hazing have been well documented by author Hank Newer ("A Chronology of Selected Hazing Incidents," http//hazing.hanknewer.com) Books by Hank Newer and available on Amazon.com include *The Hazing Reader* (2004), *Wrongs of Passage: Fraternities, Sororities, Hazing, and Binge Drinking* (2002) and *High School Hazing: When Rites Become Wrong* (2002).

For other information about this subject or to find related books available, go to StopHazing.org or KidsHealth.org, http://www.menstuff.org/issues/byissue/hazing.html,

http://privateschool.about.com/cs/students/a/hazing1.htm., www.insidehazing.com, www.linkcrew.com and library.cqpress.com. For an Alfred University research study on hazing, see www.alfred.edu/hs%5Fhazing.

RELIGION AND CHRISTIAN LIFE

SHAMEFUL TRADITIONS

Originally submitted to WELS Historical Institute Journal
*May, 2006 as a Letter to the Editor, (understandably not published)
No reply was received.*

"Lost" Traditions

In your "From the Editor" page (April, 2006), you asked for comments and suggestions about a series of vignettes about Northwestern College you are planning for future issues of the Journal. I am a charter member of *WELS Historical Institute Journal* and have long appreciated the value of preserving the past and the articles of this fine publication. The vignette concept is a good one. However, I was bothered and disappointed by the "Lost Tradition" segment. You seemed to play down or dismiss the barbaric practices of initiations as harmless. Of the "swat on the seat of the pants" and the "blindfold tricks" you state "none of which were harmful." That is not true; also, it is not a pleasant experience to have people laugh at you for appearing stupid, or left in the countryside to get lost. You say no one was hurt by this initiation except for "the ego". Wouldn't it be better to substitute the word ego with self-esteem? Humiliating others is harmful, not only to the one being initiated, but also to those who enjoy inflicting the swats and seeing others humiliated. Besides, those of us who have resided in campus dormitories know how some immature men have often exceeded any guidelines.

Administration Involvement in Traditions

You stated this was "part of the program" at Northwestern and that the faculty had knowledge of it. Unfortunately, that was very true. The angriest letter I ever wrote to anyone was one to Northwestern College about the excesses of initiations at Northwestern. This was back in the 1960s. One of the students that I had taught in grade school and encouraged for the ministry entered Northwestern and was forced to drink cod liver oil until he threw up. I could add more. How could future church workers enjoy seeing this freshman throw up? The letter I received from Northwestern in response justified initiations as something that makes kids tough for the ministry. I think a better word for tough in this case would be to desensitize. Do we really want our church workers to be insensitive?

Eradicating Shameful Traditions

While initiations are used by tough gangs to create a gang mentality, and that practice is used by other organizations for the same reason, I believe that any benefits of cohesion are far outweighed by the harmful effects. Furthermore, the reputation of Northwestern and the Synod has been hurt by this callousness for the feelings of others. That is a terrible tradition. History seems to bear out traditions, especially in the church, have a way of becoming acceptable doctrine. Unfortunately, initiation has become deeply rooted among us and is difficult to eradicate. Fortunately, Martin Luther College in New Ulm has made great stride in moving to a more evangelical approach towards incoming students -- teaching students not to cater to the human flesh that delights in the discomfort of others. Instead students are taught to respect each other in dignified ways. This is a good Christian tradition.

There are some traditions that are better off dropped and forgotten! Hopefully the *WELS Historical Institute Journal* will not publish any more vignettes that justify initiations or hazing and pass this off as harmless.

Frederick Wulff is a retired professor of MLC and resides in New Ulm, MN. Comments may be directed to fredwulff@newulmtel.net

For more information about this subject or to find related books available, go to StopHazing.org or KidsHealth.org http://www.menstuff.org/issues/byissue/hazing.html,

http://privateschool.about.com/cs/students/a/hazing1.htm

SOCIOLOGY WITH AN "S" (LIKE IN SIN)

Originally published in *The Lutheran Educator*,
volume 46, number 2, December 2005

Most of us teachers have taken a sociology course sometime or another. More than likely these courses have helped us better understand society. A number of years ago, I wrote a symposium paper touching on how sociology can be useful for classroom teachers (Wulff, "Sociology," DMLC Symposium: Equipping the Saints for Citizenship Through the Social Studies, 1990). Helpful as they may be, sociological "insights" have limitations, especially if they ignore the basic nature of human beings, or simply put, do not acknowledge the concept of sinful behavior in individuals. Dianna Fishbein, Professor of Criminology, says: "There is a growing knowledge that we are not going to solve any problem in society using just sociology" (*Scientific American* March, 1995). True, and we might add that there is a need for a biblical understanding of human nature.

Individual Responsibility and Sin

The danger is that instead of insisting on personal responsibility for actions or accountability from individuals, we push blame for shortcomings off onto society or environment in the name of sociology. In a quest to foster greater self-esteem, many offer excuses and avoid the "S" word. The order of service found in Christian Worship, whereby we regularly confess our sins, is clearly not in sync with most sociologists. The problem of shifting blame to others with little personal accountability can have a corrosive effect on both individuals and society. Instilling "self esteem" surely has a place in dealing with people. We want them to feel good about themselves, but the concept has been perverted by many modern educators — to make people feel good in situations where admonition is needed.

Institutions, Providence and Sin

One sociological paradigm, the structural-functional analysis, basically holds that all institutions in society evolve and work according to natural forces that benefit society. It stresses the importance of the institutions of family, marriage, and the government, but sees them as institutions that merely evolved because of functional societal needs. We would modify this: God created and instituted them out of his divine love and wisdom. Stable families are extremely important. Parents have been instructed: "to train a child in the way he should go and when he is old he will not turn from it" (Proverbs 22:6). This may seem narrow minded and restrictive because we allegedly are imposing our values on children, but Christian parents want the best for their children. We are strict lest our offspring become as the children of Eli (I Samuel 2:12-22), but we do this with kindness and fairness so that we do not exasperate our children. In a loving way, parents bring up their children in the training and instruction of the Lord (Ephesians 6:4).

The Marriage Institution and Sin

The institution of marriage also must be honored as more than an evolved tradition.

Individuals should be held accountable for co-habitation outside of marriage, even though society might now accept fornication as normal and natural. Unfortunately, even among some Christian families, "shacking up" is becoming respectable. Sin should be called a sin to stop this epidemic. Scripture is clear: "Marriage should be honored by all, and the marriage bed kept pure, for God will judge the adulterer and all the sexually immoral" (Hebrews 13:4). Marriage should not be looked upon as only a quaint tradition that developed over time.

Dysfunctions and Sin

Under the structural-functional analysis, even the dysfunctions contribute to the well being of society because they bring about cohesion as people rally to counter the dysfunction. This fits into the evolution mode, but it is really God who directs history, and we call the dysfunctions sin. For example, in the Old Testament story of Joseph, his brothers sought evil against him, but the outcome was used for good to "save many people alive" (Genesis 45: 4-8). Of course, this did not excuse the sin of the brothers. As Christians, we know "that in all things God works for the good of those who love him, who have been called according to his purpose" (Romans 8:28). God does direct all events, even "dysfunctions," to work for our well-being and his kingdom.

Deviant Behavior and Sin

As defined by sociologists, "deviant behavior" is behavior that is a recognized violation of cultural norms, but the reality that the definition of alleged deviant behavior is not held the same by all makes it complicated. Crime, the violation of formally enacted law, is considered "formal deviance" and therefore criminal behavior. That makes sense.

However, there is behavior that Christians should call deviant because it violates God's law and Christian norms. Just because something is lawful, does not mean we are permitted to participate in such "lawful" actions. Sin is sin. Serial divorces may be legally recognized, but the practice is sinful and demeans the institution of marriage.

Abortion performed where the mother's life is not threatened, but done just out of convenience, takes away the life of a child and is sinful. Pornographic material and obscene language are liberally permitted by law, but are not permissible in Christian homes. Scripture clearly says that out of our mouths should not come both "praise and cursing," and we must rid ourselves of "filthy language" (James 3:10 and Colossians 3:8). In a Christian community swearing and filthy language are serious deviant activities.

Cultural Differences and Sin

According to the definition of sociologists, cultural differences can be seen as deviance. Each particular culture determines what may or may not be right. A prevailing attitude is that if people are tolerant or understanding, they will respect cultural differences and not impose personal cultural standards on others. That seems to make sense, but not always. For example, when people from Southeast Asia moved into Minneapolis, there were instances where adult males married young underage girls. Should this be tolerated because it is acceptable in another society? When males of the Amazonian rainforest severely beat their women as a matter of routine, should we avoid judgment?

Muslim societies in eastern Africa force young girls to submit to female genital mutilation. In some places of the world women who have been raped are murdered by relatives because they "brought shame upon the family." Early Spanish missionaries to South America have been unfairly criticized for stopping heart-snatching sacrifices. Human sacrifices are wrong. Sin is sin and should be called sin. In the Old Testament, when children were sacrificed to Molech, God condemned the practice and told people of the community not to "close their eyes" (Leviticus 20:3-4).

Of course many deviances are just a matter of informal differences. People are considered different or deviant because they wear different styles of clothing, use tattoos or other body ornamentations, and so on. Some cultures are quite different from our own and yet have beautiful customs that may be enjoyed and even emulated.

Differences are not necessarily wrong. We Christians often call these differences from our accepted informal norms adiaphora — things that are neither commanded nor prohibited. However, where Scripture clearly instructs about wrongdoing it is a totally different matter.

Peer Pressure and Sin

Actually, Christians may be called deviant, according to the sociological definition, because we are different and do not always accommodate some cultural norms that are popular. Their peers may call Christian young people weirdoes or nerds if they are not comfortable in the world of drugs and sex. Scripture says that while we are in the world, we should not conform to the ways of the world (Romans 12:1-2). In this sense we should welcome the word deviant. We are a peculiar people "holy to the Lord our God—children of God" (Deuteronomy 14:1,2). For that we are not ashamed.

Group Behavior and Sin

The social-conflict paradigm stresses the exploitative nature of society. This approach is generally negative and views life in society as a struggle between the powerful and the vulnerable. From a Christian perspective, we note that mankind is certainly by nature exploitative. Materialistic people often take advantage of the helpless. Majority ethnic groups throughout history have often subordinated minorities, and unfortunately, probably always will, because of the ultimate root of man's sinful nature. Society needs safeguards against this. We Christians need also look at this on the individual level, not just the "they" as if advocating some kind of group guilt. Do we as individuals treat minorities in a way, as Luther expressed it, by being a Christ to our neighbors?

There is another side to this. Do those individuals within an oppressed group blame individuals who may not be responsible for their plight, like the local cop on the beat or a happenstance social worker? On an international level, how many innocent hostages did terrorists behead or how many random bus passengers were blown up because of a larger conflict? These are individual acts of murder. War crimes like those committed by individuals under the Nazis, or more recently the Serb nationalists, should not be dismissed under the blanket excuse of following military orders. "It is mine to avenge, I will repay," said the Lord (Romans 12:19). Every individual is responsible for his own sins.

Genes and Sin

The sociobiology paradigm explores the biological basis of social behavior. The modern catalyst of sociobiology research is Edward O. Wilson, who taught entomology at Harvard. He wrote his own textbook, *Sociobiology: The New Synthesis* (1975). His premise is that genes and evolution have shaped not just our bodies but our behavior as well. Controversy over this research erupted and protest demonstrations followed. Wilson was accused of encouraging the practices of sterilization, genocide, racism, and sexism. Another sociobiology perspective comes from James Q. Wilson, author of *Crime and Human Nature*. He maintains that there is an important link between heredity and criminal behavior, and that there is strong evidence of genetic transmission of human behavior.

Sociobiology makes some sense in that all people have the same human origin in Adam and Eve, and all have inherited a sinful nature. However, sin is not essentially a biological transmission. The sinful nature exists at a level deeper than cell structures and genetic codes. All humans are equally sinful no matter what distinctions appear in our DNA blueprints. Each sinner may have particular propensities toward particular sins, but all are fully corrupted by sin itself. Scripture declares: "every inclination of [the human] heart is evil from childhood" (Genesis 8:21). "There is no difference, for all have sinned and fall short of the glory of God" (Romans 3:23). Christ—not gene therapy—is the answer to our sin. As to weaknesses we exhibit in respect to specific sins, Christians are not fatalistic or deterministic as though helplessly trapped. By the grace of God, we can fight our sinful nature, fortified with help from loved ones, treatment from professionals, and most importantly, upheld by the Word of God.

Environment and Sin

Most sociologists somewhat accept the environmental/nurture approach— which emphasizes the role of nurture. E. O. Wilson (not to be confused with James Q. Wilson) defended himself from the onslaught of criticism by saying human nature is the product of both genetics and the environment. In the old argument between nature and nurture, the latter now draws our attention, that human behavior is frequently learned and shaped by the social world around us. How much are we products of our environment? Our families, schools and churches are important positive influences in shaping our behavior for the betterment of society and ourselves. Parents should provide a stable home life for their children. Teachers should modify their classrooms and teaching methods to create an atmosphere that benefits children of different abilities and learning styles. Teachers must help their students to cope with problems which stem from a changing environment much more difficult than we, or our parents, encountered — like continuous exposure to violence in movies and on TV, a prevailing instant gratification mentality, more broken homes, abusive parents, easily accessible illicit drugs, etc. The environment is important. Unfortunately, some sociologists provide too much fodder to help explain away individual shortcomings. Sinful mankind looks for excuses, and has since the beginning of time. However, people should be held accountable for their actions! In today's society, we offer a myriad of defenses to justify unacceptable behavior. In San Francisco, a murderer used as a defense that he was under the influence of Twinkies. The National Council Against Health Fraud (NCAHF) believes that misinformation is presently used to exploit the popular belief that crime and violence are products of improper diet. Scientifically trained health professionals reject that belief as unfounded (NCAHF Position Paper on Diet and Criminal Behavior; see also G. Gray and L. Gray, "Diet and Juvenile Delinquency," *Nutrition Today*, May/June, 1983).

The culture of victim-hood has trial lawyers coming out of the woodwork for every misdeed crying out that someone else or something else is culpable. Neighborhoods tear down so-called "bad" houses because crack had been sold there. Folly! Bad people sell illegal drugs, not bad buildings! A lawyer once commented that his client, who had hired a thug to put another ice skater out of an important competition event, was herself a victim. He was quoted as saying that a psychiatrist would find "the real cause" (boyfriend, mother, childhood, whatever) for her misconduct. When children underachieve at school parents often blame the teacher, the school, racism, the budget crunch, the peer group, television, etc., but almost never the child who neglects the daily assignments. We know from our own experiences, if we are honest, the reason we may not have done well in some course(s) at school really boiled down to our own attitudes. Ultimately we must teach the children individual responsibility and call sin a sin. When individuals acknowledge sin, they need to modify their behavior and appreciate forgiveness. People are not prisoners of their environment but controllers of the environment. Subdue the earth and rule over it (Genesis 1:28). Life is a challenge that calls for individual responsibility.

Conscious Choices and Sin

The last sociological approach to be considered here involves the symbolic-interaction paradigm, which views society as a highly variable product of the continuous interaction of individuals in various settings. One aspect of symbolic-interaction holds that people are not just social beings manipulated or shaped by the social world — that we are not just puppets in an over socialized conception of the human being. The sociologist George Mead recognized the power of society to act on human beings, but he also strongly argued that human spontaneity and creativity cause human beings to make choices for themselves. Another sociologist, Peter Burger, has made some thoughtful observations. He states "unlike the puppets, we have the possibility of stopping in our movements, looking up and perceiving the machinery by which we have been moved." We are choosing sinful behavior when we commit wrongdoing. As Christians we believe the Holy Spirit gives us strength to deal with the world and our flesh. It is often said that faith can move mountains. With St. Paul we acknowledge that we "can do everything through him who gives [us] strength" (Philippians 4:13).

Absolution and Sin

We choose sin, but God tells us: "You did not choose me, but I chose you" (John 15:16). How comforting this is that God chose us from eternity that we might receive the adoption of sons. Then, entirely by grace, Christ took upon himself all our sins and made them his responsibility (John 3:16). "Greater love has no one than this, that one lay down his life for his friends" (John 15:13). That is how much God loves us, and that is what gives us real self-esteem. Humans are a special creation of God. We are the crown of creation! God has called us to be the salt of the earth, to be his people. Unlike the animals, we make conscious decisions. Do not use "sociological factors" to explain away sin. Sin should not be taken lightly. It is our sin that nailed Christ to the cross.

Insist on personal responsibility for sinful behavior. Let us add an "S" for sin in our sociological outlook!

SPEAKING OUT

SOCIOLOGY PRESENTATION

Frederick Wulff

Religion Social Studies Symposium, DMLC, October 4-6, 1990

Southeastern Wisconsin District

Shoreland Lutheran High School 1992 Spring Teachers' Conference

Introduction

Sociology may be defined as the scientific study of society and the social activity of human beings. The roots of sociology go back to the Enlightenment of late eighteenth century Europe. The intellectual movement of the time was very humanistic. It emphasized the ideas of progress and a profound belief in the ability of human beings to solve their problems. The scientific study of social life was a logical extension of those two currents. Sociology is in vogue today. Most colleges and universities not only have introduction courses to sociology, but offer higher level courses in such areas as Marriage and Family, Deviance, Medical Sociology, Research Methods, Population, Sociology of Change, Sociology of Religion, Urban Studies, Aging, and others. No doubt many of these sociological areas are of concern for us educators or educators to be. Yet, I would like to state from the onset that I am not advocating that the subject sociology be added as a formal subject taught in our elementary Lutheran schools. I am, however, advocating that teachers to enhance the teaching of social studies can use sociology as a tool. Although sociology may be of value to us it also has its limitations.

The Limitations and Value of Sociology

Sociology is a science, and as such, scientific method and measurements are the norm. The goal of sociology is the discovery of social laws on the basis of which predictions may be made. But sociology, like any science, has not been able to provide answers or give meaning to the most central human needs and questions. Sociology remains particularly helpless in the face of the ultimate questions! "Why and to what end?" Our Christian beliefs offer us the comforting sense that all human social experiences, even those of the ungodly, ultimately must serve God's purpose.

God's Word gives us truths that we accept simply because we operate with the premise his Word is Truth. Sociology, as a science, operates under the assumption that absolute truth cannot be fully known and all conclusion s are only tentative. Yet, for us Christians, truths as expressed in the Bible are the final authority and do not have to be checked with scientific studies or reinforced by scientific proof. Cultural traditions and social assumptions, however, may legitimately be open to sociological study by Christians as well as others. "Christian" sociology is a general orientation and not an explicitly theory. As Christians who study sociology we can gain from sociological studies and the skills employed by that science.

Sociology does not give us THE answers, especially as to the meaning of life, but sociological insights may help us better understand society both past and present. For example, sociological studies of the trends in the divorce rates suggest that changes in society and the family are closely related, or that suicide rates are higher or lower for various categories of people at different times. As Christians we naturally resist the idea that we act in socially patterned ways or that social forces guide us in certain directions. We Christians recognize that human beings do have considerable autonomy and are responsible for their actions, but we also can concede somewhat that we are affected by the world around us -- we are deeply affected by the values, beliefs, and patterns of behavior that characterize the society in which we live. The world has always offered a way of life that may not be consistent with Christian values. This was true for the children of Israel, the saints of the New Testament era, and is still true for us Christians in the society of today. Granted, God's Word is our starting point and only sure guide to understanding the basic nature of humans and human behavior, but a study of sociological patterns can be a useful study, even with its limitations.

To understand social institutions and human culture, sociologists generally use four theoretical approaches or paradigms: (1) structural functional analysis (2) social-conflict analysis (3) natural or biological analysis, and (4) the symbolic interaction analysis. None of them, or any combination of them, is entirely satisfactory. Our unique Christian orientation offers us an added perspective as we examine each paradigm.

The Social-Conflict Paradigm

Many sociologists support a social-conflict paradigm that stresses the exploitative nature of society. This approach is generally negative and views life as a struggle between the powerful and the helpless. From a Christian perspective, we could add that certainly man is by nature sinful and exploitative. Sinful people do exploit others. We Christians too have been affected by sin and are susceptible to a narrow materialistic outlook just as those of self-seeking individuals who take advantage of the weak. Actually, the devil works overtime among us simply because we are God's people. We should see these flaws in ourselves as well as others who run roughshod over the disadvantaged. Take an example. Our conservative nature often places us on the side of those in positions of power and this perspective may cause us to label those who challenge the current status quo as troublemakers. In some cases this may be true, but it may also be that those in power positions practice injustice and we who refuse to look at the problems often prolong the problems by our passivity. Sometimes a social conflict explanation makes sense. A case in point could well be the civil rights conflict of the 50s and 60s in Mississippi. According to the social-conflict paradigm the blacks were deprived of their civil rights by a powerful and unjust social order. The blacks were being exploited, yet conservatives often saw it differently. This view has the civil rights activists who set up black registration drives as the ones creating turmoil. However, the social-conflict paradigm offers a reasonable thesis that the real conflict was caused by those who denied blacks their constitutional rights. Those white segregationists who were in power positions defied the 14th Amendment and federal court rulings when they deprived blacks of voting privileges through acts of violence and intimidation. Even within the family we may see examples of the abuse of power and again we may take the side of those who exploit their positions of power. We may want to look the other way to avoid confrontation and pretend that spouses or children are not sometimes victims of abuse. Fortunately there were some early Christians who did recognize the existence of abuse from those in positions of power within the family. For example, from 1649 to 1680 the Puritans of colonial Massachusetts enacted the first laws anywhere in the world against wife beating and "unnatural severity" to children. (See Elizabeth Pleck, *Domestic Tyranny: The Making of American Social Policy Against Family Violence From Colonial Times to the Present*, Oxford Press, 19487)

While we may agree in some cases with the exploitative conclusions reached by the social-conflict sociologists, it is for a different reason than logic or sociological studies. Scripture teaches us that all problems in society throughout history have their ultimate roots in sin and sinful nature. Christians accord greater validity to biblical images of human nature and social order than the findings of social and behavioral scientists. While science has much to teach us, we have an added advantage because of our Scriptural insights into the nature of the world and therefore of society. Our consciousness of human sin does not make us fatalistic. We are not as those who see no hope. We also know that the Holy Spirit can and does work in individuals in society bringing about change that cannot be explained through natural means. We also know that all positions of authority are not exploitative. Quite the contrary, government and parental authority have been instituted by God for our welfare and security. Truly they are intended to be blessings. This thought leads us to another paradigm, this one quite positive.

The Structural-Functional Paradigm

The structural-functional school of sociologists maintains that all institutions in society naturally work for the welfare of society. Even the dysfunctions, they maintain, contribute because they bring about cohesion in society. Members of society rally together to counter crime or objectionable behavior. We could certainly add that we Christians know that ultimately all things work together for good to those who love God - even though outward appearances may seem to show just the contrary. Many of the social institutions that we find in society are really gifts of God and not just social arrangements. We know that God has wisely created the family as the foundation of society. He has instituted government for the wellbeing of society and order in the world. Yet, though the structural-functional sociologist acknowledge the positive side of social institutions, they tend too see the institutions of families, marriage, and government only as having merely evolved because of functional societal needs. We know that God created and instituted them out of his divine love and wisdom.

The Natural or Biological Paradigm

The natural analysis stresses cultural ecology and sociobiology. Both emphasize that human culture is created within the natural world. Cultural ecology explores the interrelationship of human culture and the physical environment (climate and natural resources). Basically this views man as only the product of his surroundings. Sociobiology explores the biological basis of social behavior. James Q. Wilson, in his book *Crime and Human Nature*, takes this view when he argues that there is an important link between heredity and behavior and maintains there is evidence of genetic transmission of human behavior. According to Christopher Jencks, "Wilson is probably the most influential single writer on crime in America, though his writings are controversial."

Wilson is not alone. Recently other scholars are saying the same thing. I believe that the major flaw in the natural analysis is that human behavior is more than a product of environment or genes. It would be too easy to absolve individuals of their wrongdoings if we blame the genes. It would be too easy to say behavior is immune to modification. Some could conclude that some races have an inferior society and others superior because of genetics. History has shown the terrible consequences that have come from this kind of logic.

Sociobiology is correct in the sense that all people have the same biological roots in Adam and Eve and that all have inherited a sinful nature. Some research has shown that alcoholic propensity may be linked to genetic makeup. Alcoholic Anonymous has endorsed this notion to help alcoholics transform from thinking their problem as a character defect into an illness. Really we all have genetic weaknesses. Our propensities toward different pitfalls vary, however. It is also true that the world and our flesh are corrupting influences, but it is equally true that we are not prisoners of our culture or biology. We can drown our sinful nature in baptism and the Word. We can survive and overcome the natural environment and our sinful nature as we creatively shape our lives by the power of the Holy Spirit. As sanctified Christians we help others in their struggles to overcome obstacles.

The Symbolic-Interaction Paradigm

The last of the four paradigms, the symbolic-interaction paradigm, views society as a highly variable product of the continuous interaction of individuals in various settings. This micro-level approach helps us to overcome the limitations of the previous three macro-level approaches. People are not just social beings manipulated or shaped by the social world. We are not just puppets in an "over-socialized" conception of the human being. The sociologist George Mead recognized the power of society to act on human beings, but he also strongly argued that human spontaneity and creativity cause human beings to continually act back on society. On this basis, the process of socialization affirms the ability of human beings to make choices for themselves. The sociologist Peter Berger has made some thoughtful observations. He says "unlike the puppets, we have the possibility of stopping in our movements, looking up and perceiving the machinery by which we have been moved." Berger sees value in a study of sociology. He states the more we are able to utilize the sociological perspective to recognize how the machinery of our society works, the freer we can be. I think we can agree that the study of sociology has practical value.

Classroom Application of Sociology

Sociology could provide an added dimension in our teaching of the social studies, especially history. It behooves us to recognize how the machinery of society works elsewhere than in our own little world. With a broader perspective our young people can be made aware of sociological trends. For example, they may see patterns among the elderly in other societies throughout history. Some societies around the world have made good use of their elderly and honored them with respect. In the past grandparents of the New England colonies contributed to society and strengthened the family. Today among industrial nations like ours, the elderly seemingly appear to be unneeded and in the way of a youth-oriented culture. Should our social studies lesson not draw attention to this pattern? In "primitive" societies elderly were cherished and honored as wise, as the keepers of valued traditions and wisdom. In some societies the amount of economic "worth" determined the amount of respect given to old people. However, we could add that Scripture, not just society, gives us clear guidelines for respecting our elders and the honor that should be accorded them. An examination of sociological observations on the aging and the particular problems of the elderly may give us insights about the elderly often overlooked in normal everyday life routine. Girded with Scripture we can draw attention to the blessings of parents and grandparents, and also of members of the extended family like aunts and uncles.

RELIGION AND CHRISTIAN LIFE

The use of sociology, often neglected by "pure" historians, has found acceptance by some recent influential historians. Professor John Garraty of Columbia draws attention in his current textbook to the social life of colonial New England. He notes that a rich family life contributed to the stability of the colony and that the absence of family life could lead to a brutish way of life. Although we know that the New England ideal was in the past, and that we cannot live the past as it was, we could vicariously share in some of their family life. This gives us opportunity to recapture intimate social history and to discuss the strengths and weaknesses of societies then and now.

As we look also at the role of women in social settings across time we gain insights from the past and learn lessons that have meanings for the present. Discrimination against women had been going on for a long time before the Seneca Falls Convention of 1848. The unfair treatment women faced may seem unbelievable to us today, but in the past many thought this treatment acceptable. This added perception of another time or another place enables us to look more critically at our own world of today to see how discrimination continues even though it may appear "acceptable."

A journey into the slave community may help us to see how family and kin helped children to survive the indignities of sl1very. Today the family still serves to assist its members as they cope in an often-tough world. Observations about slavery before the industrial age may lead us to see the value of earlier family life with a father in the home and the family operating more as a cooperative unit. When fathers left the family for the workplace, there was a void. Recent studies indicate that the father's role is crucial to caring children, that paternal involvement with young children was the single strongest parent-related factor in adult empathy and compassion (26 year study by Richard Koestner and Carol Franz). Earlier studies have linked the father's involvement to higher self-esteem, better grades and more sociability. But, the Koestner-Franz report goes on to say, single parents are not doomed if they provide very responsive adult help. We ourselves as teachers may find ourselves needed as "significant others" when we work with children who are lacking important family members. A classroom study of the family in society could lead to some valuable discussions.

Sociologists note that family ties are often weaker in the cities and that neighborhood ties are often impersonal. As we teach social studies about urbanization there will be an opportunity to note the marked change in the character of social life in the cities and the need for common identity and collective goals, and how the urban church might assist people alone in the crowded cities by offering them personal ties within a congregation of brothers and sisters in Christ.

Spiritual Values

In contemporary American society we have a social climate that stresses individualism, the "me first" and materialistic goals of the world, rather than a goal of service to others. We may wish to consider the theme of a timely book entitled *Habits of the Heart*. This timely book by Robert Bellah, Richard Madsen, William Sullivan, Ann Swindler and Steven Tipton is based on a massive five-year sociological study. The authors analyze one of today's central moral dilemmas: the conflict between our fierce individualism and our urgent need for community and commitment to one another. Understandably, Bella's book is used in a cooperative effort by both the sociology and the religion departments of Concordia College in Moorhead, Minnesota. Obviously our ultimate source of authority on the danger of self-centered materialism comes from the Bible. Yet sometimes our society is so close to us and the values of our society are so much a part of us that we do not see the dangers of materialism that God warns us against. The impact of religion on society and society on religion is an area worthy of study. It would be easy to assume that society has shaped religion. We live a nation of materialism and it is true that some well-known church evangelists (like Jimmy and Tammy Baker) have literally been converted to materialism, as is evident in money motivated messages and lavish lifestyles. Some lament that the spiritual values of Christianity have been muted and our society has becomes quite secular. Yet, we could also argue there still are faithful Christians and that the powerful Gospel is still at work and effective in society.

Cultivating A Wider View

The understanding and appreciation of other cultures is a desirable outcome for social studies. Sociologists say that if we really want to understand people in another society we must view that society in its own normative terms. This is difficult. We naturally tend to judge other cultures by the standards of our own culture, revealing our subjectivity. All too often we view reality only in accordance with our own localistic viewpoint and we become very parochial. Hence our tolerance for diversity may be considerably narrowed and even our imaginations conform to the existing system. Our sheltered existence may make us view other cultures as not normal or inferior. Although we may not be fully aware that we are viewing life through a fixed lens, our outlook may be so set in cultural traditions that we hinder our own ability to communicate with others of different cultural backgrounds. It could appear to others that we are standoffish. The historian Paul Boyer believes that German immigrants were perceived as being aloof because of their tight socially knit communities. Although the newcomers were admired for their industriousness, they were disdained for their clannish psychology. The German immigrants did not perceive themselves this way and responded by becoming even more clannish. (Paul Boyer, et. el., *The Enduring Vision*, D.C. Heath, 1990)

A sociological perspective might lead us to ask if both the German-Americans and the native-born Americans viewed each other through fixed lenses. As Christians, whose primary concern is communicating the Gospel to all people, we would find a sociological perspective helpful to combat an ethnocentricity that hinders our outreach into another culture. If we realize there are more "social realities" than our traditional one, we become broader in our outlook. We may feel less secure and comfortable in a world where we recognize more "social realities," but our true security and comfort comes not from cultural traditions but from the stability of God's absolute truths - truths that transcend cultural differences. Our consummate social relationship is that Christ lives in us and we in Christ.

Absolute Values

As Christian teachers we know that there are universal ethical standards whereby all social systems can be evaluated. We do take issue with those who speak of ethics as relative and challenge our position of Christian absolutism. While we acknowledge that humans create a collective sense of reality, including ethical reality, a Christian perspective refuses to assume that all ethics are mere human creations, and hence relative. We will take issue with those who see marriage or sexual preference as "lifestyles" subject to "alternative" possibilities. Where God has spoken out on the issue, we will follow his directives. We will speak out and at the same time we exhibit the love and kindness that God has shown to us sinners.

Considering the massive social problems in society today, and we live in this world, sociology from a Christian perspective can be of genuine benefit to us teachers. Worthwhile reading for teachers is Richard Perkins Looking *Both Ways, Exploring the Interface Between Christianity and Sociology.* (Grand Rapids, 1987), The author warns us that sociology and Christianity do not naturally get along, but he also encourages us to understand the social world from several perspectives simultaneously. He believes that Christians can benefit by learning what sociologists have to offer and vice versa.

We Christian teachers are naturally interested in studies of the family, especially since the family has undergone dramatic changes recently.

A good starting point is the Bible itself and Bible aids. Edith Deen, *Family Living in the Bible*, (Pyramid Book, New York, 1969) may be helpful. Teacher Gerald Kastens of Lake Mills, Wisconsin has written a paper for the Board for Parish Services entitled "Family Life Ministry Project." In this project he developed the Scriptural foundations concerning family and family-life ministry. A primary grade level (K-3) filmstrip series "God's Plan for Families" is available for rental from Northwestern Publishing House. The three filmstrips (Families are God's Plan, Families Work Together and Friendly to Others) are in color and last 7-8 minutes each

CIVILITY

Originally A Letter to the Editor
New Ulm *Journal* (printed) 2012

Petty Nitpicking Politics

Ah, to have politics with civility. This doesn't come easily. Even the early leaders of the Republic often characterized rivals in a rather rough manner. However, the elusive goal of being civil in politics is worth great effort. Recently the level of crudeness for depicting the political opposition seems to have reached the bottom of the pit. Some e-mails that are circulating are unbelievably wicked. Newspapers and TV stations seek out little frivolous flaws in political figures or minor errors in speeches and blow them up as newsworthy. Remember when Dan Quayle was hit for his misspelling of the word potato. David Letterman said he himself was not aware that potato did not end in e, but he did know the word imbecile does. As of late, prominent women especially have been under the microscope for derision. Some newspapers are very selective in choosing whom to target. One can only guess the motivation is to make those of a different gender or perspective look inept or stupid. And then how often do we read about positions of individuals being brushed off as being racist, for no other reason than to stifle legitimate debate. Why is it that we must resort to name calling and character assassination of those whom we disagree?

Polarization

The rhetoric can be downright nasty. In a democratic form of government disparate views can and should be debated, so that reasonable ground may be reached in the interest of achieving what is best for public welfare. Political parties have different approaches for solving problems. They may have strong feelings about the best way to govern, but that does not mean it has to be construed as a battle between good and evil. When the opposition is unfairly painted as satanic, compromise becomes difficult if not impossible. This polarization also discourages reaching across the aisle. A stalemated, do-nothing government is the result and we are all the worse off because of a backlog of unfinished business.

Character Assassination

Presidents make big targets. Previously President George W. Bush was personally and viciously attacked; currently President Barack H. Obama is facing the same kind of venom and with the same intensity. More than likely, neither of them has horns. The examples of slander on all levels of government are endless. Where is the concept of the honorable opposition? Those who hold office do have an honorable profession. There are some good respectable people in government who take their responsibilities seriously.

Fight a Good Fight

What impression do we give the upcoming generation when we relentlessly besmirch reputations, ignore laws that we don't like or to physically threaten persons in government when they pass legislation we find difficult to accept? Understandably, we have strong feelings about politics, but why not vent them in a constructive way by expressing our views on real issues– and working within the system?

Think twice before forwarding nasty e-mails void of worthy substance, whether from the left or the right. Pass on to others that which is informative and verifiable. For those of a religious persuasion, pray for both parties that they seek wisdom and understanding.

Be actively engaged in the political dialogue, but be civil and respect the office of each elected official regardless of party. That's the way our governmental system is supposed to work. Ah, to have politics with civility.

Frederick Wulff, New Ulm

"CHRISTIAN POLITICS": THE BEST FOR BOTH WORLDS

Originally published in The Lutheran Educator, *volume 47, number 1, 2006*

A Fundamental Lesson from the Word

Most of us would agree that the deteriorating American culture needs a fix. The growing acceptance of disrespectful behavior, the prevailing use of obscene language, the drug scene and the ugly face of violence alarm us. It seems the church should do more to curb the ills of society. Well, a note of caution is in place here and a review of the doctrine of the Two Kingdoms. God does not intend for the church to rule a worldly government. The roles that God has given the church and the state are separate and distinct. He has given His Means of Grace to the church to bring salvation to all people; whereas, the role of the state is to govern society with the power that resides in natural law. We

Christians have dual membership, but we understand that the roles of church and state must not be confused. We should "give to Caesar that which is Caesar's, and unto God that which is God's" (Matthew 22:21). The church has no direct role over the state; there is no prescribed left or right strategy to rule. However, as individual Christians, we are to be the salt of the earth. Thus, as sanctified Christians, we should naturally be well-informed and active citizens. It follows then that individual Christians will be valuable assets to any government

Learning from History

If we can learn anything from history, it is the painful lesson that stems from a confusion of the church/state roles. Starting in the 4th century, under Constantine, Christianity became a sanctioned religion of the state. By the end of the century, the secular kingdom was wielding the keys that Christ had committed to the church. The sad years of papal power in secular matters are all too familiar to us. During the reign of the Renaissance popes, Luther's powerful proclamation of the Word shook the worldly kingdom and power of Rome and the shameful state of the church. The churches of the Reformation, freed from worldly papal power, and then wrestled with church/state relations in a new setting. Article 28 of the Augsburg Confession wisely stated: "The power of the church and the civil power must not be confused." Unfortunately the governments under both the Church of Rome and the Lutherans (Peace of Augsburg, *cuius regio, eius religio*) persecuted non-members in their regions. The Anabaptists, who were not a power player, gave up on what they perceived as the fallen church and the fallen state and disavowed the power of the government over them.

John Calvin's misconception of a Christian nation (commonwealth) is derived from his view of the church and state functioning as a firm partnership. Calvin placed more emphasis on externals than Luther in this respect. He used the state as an arm of the church whereby the magistrates helped him impose church rule in Geneva –to establish his

"City of God." In this plan, the elders of the church regulated outward behavior and had oversight over the lives of everyone. Through their mission zeal, the Calvinists (the Reformed Christian churches) spread the Gospel throughout the world and along with it, this concept of the Christian commonwealth. A shade of this view of Christian government or Christian nation is still evident in the thinking of the Religious Right. This is not meant to be a harsh judgment on the spirituality of those Christians. No doubt many of them are sincere Christians, but we still note that they have a fuzzy view of church/state relations in their concept of a Christian nation.

Politics as a Worthy Vocation

Politics is achieving the possible. We live in a sinful world with people of all kinds of religious beliefs, or unbelief. We have to get along, in spite of differences, and that requires pragmatism and cooperation. In Iraq, hopefully that would mean Kurds, Sunni, Shiites and secularists, with a sprinkle of Christians thrown in, will have to try to live together in the same geographic area. Some form of working government is necessary, because the alternative is civil war or anarchy. Throughout the world God provides government (which achieves the possible), as a stabilizing influence for order in a disorderly world: "Everyone must submit himself to the governing authorities, for there is no authority except that which God has established. The authorities that exist have been established by God" (Romans 13:1).

Here in the United States, the task of sharing participatory power does not seem so daunting as in the Near East. Still the work is challenging. Throughout our history we have had a number of selfless statesmen who have served for the greater public welfare. Christians, too, can serve in this noble endeavor of public service, often in a role of peacemaker among the factions, to achieve the best possible for the greater good. The desired effect is not always perfect. Jimmy Carter once said he personally opposed abortion for unwanted pregnancies at a time when many in his own party disagreed with him, but he sought the best possible alternative -- parental notification guidelines, waiting periods against hasty actions and adoption options. His actions saved lives of some children, though not all, who were helpless in their mothers' wombs.

Serving "Our" Constituency

Within the Church, we can insist on the supremacy of the Scripture, which had been given to the Church, but we must realize the government of secular society rules on the basis of natural law. The government serves a very broad constituency, many of who are of different religious or philosophical persuasions. Politicians have to appeal to coalitions among diverse people to support various platforms within a political framework. In our country, we basically have a two party system, with a third party occasionally playing a role; and then within those parties we can further delineate centrists, left of center and right of center. The world of politics involves teamwork among heterogeneous groupings.

I would venture that if we constructed a sociogram and placed our church members as dots on a political spectrum, we might see some discernable pattern between rural churches and urban or inner city churches. We might be surprised to see some of our members outside the clusters of dots. Our commission to preach the Gospel to everyone has brought in, and hopefully continues to bring in, members that do not fit into the typical socio-economic framework of our established congregations.

Even within an average congregation, parents of our students have diverse outlooks. It is not realistic to expect everyone in a congregation, let alone a Synod, to have the same political viewpoints on all issues. Besides, political parties and political candidates themselves can, and do, change positions on various issues, often between the primaries and the general elections. As Christians, we may agree on some issue, like respecting the sanctity of life. But, even here, we may diverge on specifics: like which wars are just wars, on rights to control gun ownership, on application of capital punishment or on choosing between the life of an endangered expectant mother and the life of the unborn child. Similarly, we may favor divergent methodologies on an acceptable social policy. The world of politics is very subjective.

Solving the Problems of Society

Should we be as the Amish or Hutterites who give up on "sinful" government and withdraw into isolated communities? Should we turn governmental affairs over entirely to the secularists to determine policy? Should we do as the Reformed and impose our religious teachings on others? Hopefully, none of the above. Rather, I suggest that we as <u>individuals,</u> as the salt of the earth, be personally involved in the political process for the best possible outcomes. Our lesson plans may well vary as how we might best be a brother to our neighbor. We might share the same concern for the elderly, the poor, the unemployed, those on the margin of society and unborn babies, but our strategies for assistance could be quite different. Some, understandably, would see the government machinery as the key provider of assistance. Yet others might stress volunteerism and plans that foster self-reliance. Some speak of faith-based initiatives. Still others favor a combination, or all of the above. We do not necessarily all find agreement. Whatever the preference, hopefully our citizenship will reflect the love of Christ in us and not manifest an indifference to those in need.

The Need for Debate and Exchange of Ideas

The lively debate between liberals and conservatives is not harmful, quite the contrary. In my over 25 years membership in the Organization of American Historians, I have thoroughly enjoyed discussions of professional papers submitted by leading historians of different persuasions.

True, polls show most historians to be political liberals, but generally the wisest are quite fair-minded toward contrary views. However, in more recent years, the post-modernist extremists have shut down scholarly debate and in its stead placed irrational nonsense. These individuals are a threat in that they will tolerate no dissenting opinions. Apparently, for some, scholarship and research count for little and any contrary view is shouted down. My fear is that the OAH is being led into a political ideology that is at odd with this prestigious organization's original purpose – the exchange of scholarly knowledge. In earlier articles, I have strongly criticized professors of this emerging fringe, not because they were left or right, but because they stifle true debate. Some of their persuasion criticized private church colleges for possessing a narrow outlook. True, many private schools do have a distinct philosophy and deeply held convictions, but for the most part, they are very civil and will allow other views to be expressed.

Seek "Honest History" Free of a Political Agenda

Many of you readers probably recall a news release a number of years ago about the professional organization THS being formed to promote "honest" history. Fed up with militant driven agendas, the undersigned switched membership from the OAH for the more balanced THS or The History Society. No doubt there are still fair-minded history professors in the OAH, but objectivity was taking a back seat. The new THS expressed their rationale for existence quite clearly in their preamble:

> The Society promotes frank debate in an atmosphere of civility, mutual respect, and common courtesy. All we require is that participants lay down plausible premises, reason logically, appeal to evidence, and prepare for exchanges with those who hold different points of view.... where other historians can exchange ideas and contribute to each other's work. (http://www.bu.edu/historic/about.html).

Along this same line, there is an interesting website for History News Network from George Mason University (hnn.us) where historians and other bloggers try to promote "honest" history. <u>Not all</u> people who blog are qualified or trustworthy, but there is some substantive food for thought within the sources. This History News Network has as objectives:

> To expose politicians who misrepresent history.
>
> To point out bogus analogies.
>
> To remind Americans of the irony of history.
>
> To put events in context.
>
> To remind us all of the complexity of history.

An example of exposing politicians, who misrepresent history and bogus analogies, was the treatment of Professor Ward Churchill of the University of Colorado. Information revealed that he lacked a PhD (usually required for tenure), lied about claiming to be a Native American to obtain his position, is charged with plagiarism and fraud, advocates violence against innocent civilians and calls the victims of 9/11 little Nazis. Native Americans groups have denounced him as an imposter for years. Yet, students of the University of Wisconsin-Whitewater gave him a standing ovation when he spoke there in 2005 as a paid speaker. Of course, we always have to ask ourselves whether freedom of speech is at stake or not. Either way, a background of discerning "honest" history will aid us in making assessments and help us be better teachers and citizens.

The Primary Role of the Church

As called Christian church workers we see the Religious Right as well meaning, but a threat to the Church as a whole, because it lures church bodies into the political arena. Their agenda is attractive because it supports so many areas of concern to us (pornography, obscenities, abortion, homosexual behavior, etc.), but history has shown how political power can detract from the mission of the church. In more recent history, one needs only look at the National Council of Churches and its political pronouncements (in this case to the left) to see how an organization can stray from the Gospel ministry. Often statements released to the press by the NCC do not reflect the views of those in the pews. The Catholic clergy in some areas of Latin America became so involved in the politics of liberation theology that the common parishioners have had to become missionaries to the clergy.

Do not sacrifice the church for politics. Jesus said," My Kingdom is not of this world" (John 18:36). For those of us in full-time Kingdom work, preaching the Gospel is paramount. Everything we say and do is subordinate to bringing others to Christ. For this is what the Lord has commanded us: "I have made you a light for the Gentiles, that you may bring salvation to the ends of the earth" (Acts 13:47). The church should avoid the pitfall of seeking world power to impose our teachings on others. Preach the Word of Reconciliation and encourage individual members to freely vote their conscience – and to be good citizens. We will then provide the best for both worlds.

Frederick Wulff is a retired MLC history/social science professor now residing in New Ulm, MN. Comments may be directed to fredwulff@newulmtel.net

RELIGION AND CHRISTIAN LIFE

DEFINING MARRIAGE AS BETWEEN A WOMAN AND A MAN

*Originally intended as a Letter to the Editor of the *
Minneapolis Star Tribune in 2012 (but not submitted)

Let's Have a Reasonable Debate on the Marriage Amendment

Public debate on any amendment is healthy, but name calling and making unwarranted assumptions about motives is not very helpful. Motives for a yes vote may have evolved from a number of factors. First we should consider the reason for the amendment in the first place. The existing law is already clear. The problem for many is that recent activist judges seem to judge not on the basis of what the law says, but to legislate from the bench and to inflict the public with their personal ideology. There are those who want the marriage definition to be as our law defines it. These people favor a yes vote to place it in the constitution to protect it from any judicial activists.

Position of Conservative Christians

Many churches, especially those who respect the authority of the Bible would like to preserve the Biblical definition. This is not being mean spirited but rather being faithful to their strongly held reverence for the Bible. Good Christians do not (or should not) have hateful feelings towards fellow citizens of different sexual orientation. We are all sinners and every one of us needs to look at our own sinful nature, but the Bible does speak clearly about marriage in a number of passages. The treatment of marriage is a matter of conscience for many individuals and they should not be dismissed as being hateful or insensitive. Many pastors are concerned that if the marriage definition is changed, activists may attempt to force them to perform same sex marriages that are contrary to Biblical teachings.

SPEAKING OUT

Positions of Sociologists

Sociologists are all over the place on conclusions about families within marriage, or shack-up arrangements, but most sociologist who wear shoes would agree that the family is the basic institution for the well being of society. Many studies show that where there is no husband (male) in the home the children suffer in school and in personal relationships, and society suffers in the long run. This is true not just in the inner city but also for society as a whole. True many wives (females), often with the help of the child's grandmother (female), attempt nobly to raise children without a father in the home. Yet, it is an uphill battle and often futile. How would a household with two fathers (male) fare? One could argue that a home is really incomplete without the mother. While it is true that many men are very caring and would exert great effort to raising children, there is some thing about a mother's love that is difficult to replace. Sociologists and others who hold these views feel that the traditional marriage and traditional family would be the best fit for a stable society. For them a yes vote on the referendum makes good sense,

Others favor a yes vote because they fear that making marriage contingent only on a loving relationship would open a can of worms. What if a person loves two people or more? A number of societies have (and still do) sanction polygamy. What if a person loves his sister or brother and wants an intimate sexual relationship (as has happened in royal families throughout history)? Some so-called sociologists go so far as to condone marriage of adults with children (both arranged and consensual) – as, unfortunately, is still practiced in a number of societies. Within all of these aberrations one could argue that there is a sincere loving relationship. But, is that enough for a marriage?

Position of Civil Rights Activists

Those who favor a no vote on the marriage amendment may also have good intentions and a loving spirit. Apparently, the *Minneapolis Star*

Tribune gives this camp its full support. Central to that position is that the right to marry cannot be separated from civil rights. Homosexuals are citizens. Perhaps civil unions would lead to a fairer solution. Civil unions, however, are not mentioned in the proposed amendment.

Hopefully the discussion does not lead to homophobia or to further discrimination against those who so often have been victims of bullies from childhood. All of us fall short of the glory of God and share the grace of God. And as well, lets hope that the discussion does not lead to dismissing people of good faith as just being hateful.

THE PARALLELS BETWEEN ISLAM AND MORMONISM

Originally published in *The Lutheran Educator*, volume 43, number 4, May 2003

A Bible class I recently attended studied the timely topic of Islam by using the text of the Qur'an (Koran) as the basis for discussion. The instructor provided valuable guidance to overflowing classes of interested students and members of the congregation. In the very first discussion session, one church member made the observation that just as Islam started with a vision(s), so did the Mormon religion of the Church of Latter Day Saints. My first reaction was that while this was true, comparing these religions is like comparing apples to oranges, especially since no one would ever expect a suicide bomber on a jihad mission to come from among our very American

Mormon neighbors. Upon further reflection, I thought that these two religions, though originating in different parts of the world in totally different cultures, and in a completely different time frame, did have parallels.

SPEAKING OUT

Known to Unknown

A fundamental axiom of educators is we should bridge that which is unfamiliar to that which is familiar. Most of us teachers live in communities that have little contact with Muslims. What little we know about the Islamic religion has reached us through the media accounts since September 11. On the other hand, we know quite a bit about the Mormons. Many of us WELS teachers have visited some of the well-publicized Mormon historic sites around the country and have been met with eager guides passing out all kinds of informational pamphlets. All of us have encountered the ubiquitous Mormon missionaries at the front door. Then too, we are acquainted with Mormon history because it is an integral part of 19th and 20th century American history found in our classroom textbooks. Starting with this common background, we could engage in a little mental exercise and make some comparisons of Islam with the Mormon religion.

Revelations/Holy Books

First of all, these two religions both believe that biblical teachings have been imperfectly preserved or understood and can be full reconstituted only through supplemental revelation. In the case of the Muslims, Muhammad felt that Jews and Christians have tampered with the Bible. Both of these religions, therefore, have their origin with visions resulting in a new alleged holy book. The revelations or visions of these two religions were brought about by an intense climate of religious strife. Muhammad (or spelled Mohammed), living at Mecca (also spelled Makkah) on a caravan route between Asia and Africa, was confronted with prevalent polytheism, along with the theological factionalism in Christendom over the person of Christ (resolved partially at a church council in 451 AD). Somewhat similarly, Joseph Smith was confronted with the factionalism of five different churches vying for members in his hometown of Palmyra. The religious strife was intensified by the fervent revival preaching of the 1820s on what was an east-west trade route from Albany to Buffalo in New York. The introductory display at the Salt Lake City Mormon Information Center on Temple Square attempts to illustrate the different factions of Christianity encountered by Joseph Smith. Smith claimed that at the age of fourteen he had already been cautioned in a vision that all existing religious beliefs were false (Ludlow, v II, 515). Three years later, he offered what he maintained was a simple alternative to the confusing proliferation of Christian sects (Ludlow, v III, 1334). Both Muhammad in 610 AD and later Smith in the Second Great Awakening had visions from angels (Gabriel to Muhammad and Moroni to Smith) that they were to become prophets of what was alleged to be the one and only true faith.

Ongoing Revelations

Both have a theology of ongoing revelations, although in the case of Islam the 23 years of visions ended with the death of Muhammad. The Koran stated, "If we abrogate a verse or cause it to be forgotten, we will replace it by a better one or one similar" (Koran 2:106). Joseph Smith said in 1842, "We believe He will yet reveal many great and important things," as confessed by Mormons in the Ninth Article of Faith. In the Mormon Church, the apostles claim to receive additional visions to revise theology, as evident by the LDS changing positions toward polygamy after an 1890 Supreme Court decision and a revelation by the Mormon President Woodruff (Ludlow, v III, 1109). More recently, in 1978 after the civil rights era, Mormon President Kimball received a revelation that reversed the prohibition of accepting Blacks into their priesthood and participating in temple ordinances (Ludlow, v II, 908). Actually, the Mormons are better at adaptation to the times than the Muslims. The Mormons firmly believe in separation of church and state with religious tolerance (Ludlow, v II, 942; v IV, 1483); but Mormons survive in the intolerant Muslim state-controlled countries like Saudi Arabia and Iran by giving their members strict instructions to refrain from any mission activity within the countries (Ludlow, v II, 902-903).

Historical Inaccuracies

Of greater significance, both religions draw upon the Apocrypha, and both have major historical inaccuracies in their sacred books. The Koran, when it refers to biblical accounts of the Old and New Testaments, is confusing and full of errors (Koran 15:26-35 and 26:23-48). References to Alexander the Great in secular history are garbled as well (Koran 18:85ff). Similarly, the Book of Mormon, published in 1830, preposterously refers to an ancient Christian history of Nephites and Lamanites in the New World before Columbus (Ludlow, v II, 804; v III,1003; v IV, 1477). The Native Americans, whom we consider the first Americans, are regarded by Mormons as descendants of the Lamanites (Ludlow, v III, 981). According to Joseph Smith, Moroni buried special golden plates at Hill Cumorah, near Palmyra in 421 AD, 1400 years before revealing the incident to him. Archeologists or historians cannot reconcile the time framework. The Bible of Christianity, in contrast, is firmly rooted in real history, and consequently there are many witnesses throughout the centuries substantiating its historical and geographical references as factually accurate.

Rapid Growth

Joseph Smith initially encountered some intense hostility from the larger community. He was persecuted so he eventually moved westward, only to be murdered by an angry mob at Nauvoo, Illinois. Muhammad's preaching angered and frightened the Meccans and some of them even plotted to kill him. In 622, Muhammad fled to the city of Medina (also spelled Madinah) where a group of people helped him. Both religions subsequently grew at a rapid pace. Mormons increased through vigorous mission activity and, initially, from a high birth rate. In the case of Islam, Muslim calif Abu Bakr and his successors pursued militancy and built an Islamic empire. Today, the two faiths are among the United States' fastest growing religions, the former through conversions and the latter through recent immigration. Unlike Mormons, the Muslims are not primarily interested in gaining converts. Reaching out to new members is hindered by their insistence that the original Arabic language of the Koran is inseparable from its message. Many people of the world, who earlier had converted in Muslim conquered regions, had done so, not so much from conversion pressure or persecution pressure, as for relief from oppressive taxation. Whatever the case, growth was phenomenal in both religions.

Schisms

Both churches, soon after their founding, had similar schisms over prophetic succession and subsequently split into two main factions. In the case of the Mormons, the main body of believers accepted the Quorum of Twelve Apostles with its president Brigham Young, while the smaller branch that rejected this affiliation and followed the lineal successor of Joseph Smith III, became the Reorganized Church of the Latter-day Saints (Ludlow, v III, 1212). In similar fashion, the followers of Muhammad splintered into two factions over prophetic succession into what are known today known as the Shiites and Sunni Muslims. The less numerous Shiites (in Iran and southern Iraq) claim allegiance to Muhammad's descendants.

Revered Shrines

Muhammad and Joseph Smith are closely associated with what became revered holy sites. Other sites significant to the founding activities or establishment of the respective religions have been made into historic shrines (Ludlow, v II, 592ff). As a study tour student or as a tourist on vacation, you may have visited many of these sites. Mormon sites include Palmyra in New York, North Omaha in Nebraska, Liberty Jail in Missouri, Nauvoo in Illinois, and the famous Mormon Tabernacle in Utah. Muslims most highly regard Mecca and Medina, but I would guess that high on the list for Islamic sites would be the Pavilion of Holy Relics in the Topkapi Palace in Istanbul. Here one may view a footprint of Muhammad, a lock of the prophet's hair, a strand of his beard, a tooth, a handwritten letter, and soil from his burial site. In Istanbul, you may have also toured Muslim mosques like the oft-visited Sultan Ahmet Mosque (Blue Mosque). Other significant mosques, like the Taj Mahal in India, and the Alhambra in Spain, are also popular shrines. Yet, both religions have very firm restrictions banning outsiders' attendance at some particular sites. The interior of the LDS Mormon Temple, or any Mormon temple for that matter, is not open to the public and only those having proper credentials of worthiness are admitted. In these temples, the living may be baptized for the dead (by proxy) and provisions made for eternal marriages, both for the living and the dead. Muslims, too, have some stringent restrictions. The entire city of Mecca, with its sacred Kaaba, is strictly off limits to non-Muslims.

Prescribed Outward Behavior

Both Islam and the Mormon Church stress work righteousness, which includes a firm prohibition of alcohol. Conformity to strictly prescribed behavior is essential to eternal salvation for both. Muhammad exhorted his followers to submit to the five pillars of Muslim obedience. Giving alms to the poor is quite important, most notably in the month of Ramadan. The Mormons are well known for charitable endeavors, above all for taking care of the economic needs of their own (Ludlow, v II, 661; v III, 113). My own personal experiences, in leading study tours through Mormon country and then later visiting Muslim countries as a tourist, were that outward behavior was extremely important to the believers of those respective religions. Joseph Smith had promoted a mutant Puritanism of sorts, derived from the influence of early New England revivalists, whereas Muhammad required total submission to Allah. Followers of both religions are repulsed by the low community standards and prevailing loose morality of our present modern society.

RELIGION AND CHRISTIAN LIFE

Views on Sin and Redemption

On the most vital issue, both religions make references to Jesus Christ as a prophet, with the Mormons, relatively speaking, treating him more favorably. Neither give Christ due credit. Interestingly enough, Mormons use the hymn text of "I Know That My Redeemer Lives" by Samuel Medley, but their interpretation of Jesus as redeemer is unique and limited (Ludlow, v IV, 1700). Muslims believe: "The messiah Jesus, the son of Mary, was no more than God's apostle... God forbid that He Himself should beget a son" (Koran 4:171). In the Muslim Koran, Christ did not rise from the dead: "They did not kill him, nor did they crucify him, but they thought they did... They did not slay him for certain" (Koran 4:156-158). The Koran further states that Christ is not God and should not be worshiped "instead of God" (Koran 3:47). Both religions maintain we have no original sin, and all people are perceived as capable of doing good and satisfying God with their behavior (Ludlow, v III, 985 and Koran 35:29,3). Mormons teach that children younger than eight are not capable of committing sin and are not held accountable for sin. They believe that "men will be punished for their own sins, and not for Adam's transgression" (Ludlow, v I, 13; v II, 673). Most alarmingly, Mormons teach "Christ's atonement gifts are conditioned upon obedience and diligence in keeping God's commandments in life's journey. The kind or nature of the resurrected body, as well as the time of one's resurrection, is affected very directly by the extent of one's faithfulness in this life"(Ludlow, v I, 84).

Materialistic Hereafter

The salvation that Muslims and Mormons believe they earn takes them to a materialistic heaven. For Muslims, God will say, "Eat and drink to your heart's content." Heaven is a fleshly paradise of delights with "dark eyed houris (virgins)" (Koran 52:15-17). For Mormons, a physical hereafter awaits them, "to experience physical sensations of all kinds" (Ludlow, v I, 401; v II, 466) and even their animals will enjoy eternal felicity praising God in languages God understands (Ludlow, v I, 42). There are, however, among Mormons degrees of glory or rewards, commensurate with the law they have obeyed. Those in the highest level and who have an eternal marriage will now have spiritual children (Ludlow, v I, 368; v II, 465). If any are judged unworthy, they are given time in hell where they learn to abide by the laws they rejected; eventually they receive a lower glory depending on the lives they had lived (Ludlow, v I, 369). It's all up to the individual. In the religion of Islam, the unworthy who do not totally submit to Allah, face real hell (Koran 4:13). Many, if not most, of the verses in the Koran threaten hellfire if your works are not sufficient. Yet, like the Apocryphal type purgatory of Mormons, in Islam a person suffers refining punishment before being received in heaven.

Conclusion

Of course these two religions have many differences besides the positions on freedom of religion and religious toleration. The topic of differences could provide fodder for a lengthy discourse. The core of all man-made religions, however, is the same. After a perusal of the Koran and the Book of Mormon, one cannot help but come away with a greater appreciation of the uniqueness of the Holy Scriptures in our Christian faith. What a contrast between manmade religions based on a futile work righteousness and a Christian's assurance of a loving God who has done it all for us. Assurance of salvation in Christ is revealed in the sure foundation of the infallible Word! With the WELS hymn writer Kurt Eggert we could sum up this love for us as "amazing grace." It is this amazing grace that prompts our expressions of appreciation to our loving God.

Amazing grace-that chose us e'r the worlds were made
Amazing grace-that sent your Son to save
Amazing grace-that robed us in your righteousness
And taught our lips to sing in glory and praise
Christian Worship 392:2

WORK CITED

Ludlow, Daniel H. ed. *Encyclopedia of Mormonism: The History, Scripture, Doctrine, and Procedures of the Church of Jesus Christ of Latter-day Saints* (4 vols.) New York: Macmillan Publishing Company, 1992.

A STRANGE JOURNEY TO BECOMING A CHURCH WORKER

This rough sketch was given to *InFocus*, a MLC publication (not published)

Family Background

The Lord truly works in mysterious ways. One would hardly expect a WELS church worker's journey to begin in an un-churched family in Detroit, a city, which at that time, was some-what a missionary outpost of the Wisconsin Synod. Yet, anything is possible with God. A mission minded WELS pastor, Reverend Wilmer Valleskey, had reached my mother and she became a member of his small church, Hope Lutheran of Detroit. Later she was baptized as an adult. My sister was stricken by polio as a teenager and spent a year in the Sigma Gama Hospital for polio victims. Pastor Valleskey visited her there and she became the second member of our family to join Hope. Eventually she went to Michigan Lutheran Seminary, DMLC, and then to Bethany Lutheran College before being assigned as a teacher to Trinity Lutheran School in Crete, Illinois. My father, a fallen away Catholic, was convinced to take an adult Bible class by this same pastor. He became the third member of our family to join Hope Lutheran. When my older brother finished his military tour of duty in Europe, he was approached by the pastor and subsequently took adult instruction classes. Soon after he became the fourth member of our family to join the church. One by one the family had come to know Christ through this Wisconsin Synod pastor.

Becoming a WELS Member

I was the last challenge for Pastor Valleskey. My very negative attitude toward churches (at that free spirit stage of my life) made me an unlikely prospect. My father told me about the adult Bible class which he had attended at Hope Lutheran. Although I had no interest in becoming a member of a church, as a high school dropout I was interested in furthering my educational background. I agreed to study the Bible as history and literature. So, at the age of twenty-three, I took the adult Bible class primarily as a critic. While attending the evening adult Bible class, I did not have any "thunderstorm" experiences, but the Spirit works wonders through the Word. I did come to know and appreciate God's Word. God led me to recycle myself by finding a way to further the Gospel message.

God's Miraculous Ways

I was an odd candidate for the teaching ministry. My educational background was quite different from most future church workers. I had taken the easy general course in public high school, but then decided to switch to the academic track in my senior year to be a lawyer. The public high school principal was annoyed by the inconvenience this might involve with scheduling and said I could not change tracks during my senior year. So I impulsively dropped out of public high school. Subsequently I was employed in electronics by the Power Equipment Company in Detroit for five years and worked my way up to a supervisor position. This in itself was a strange situation, since supervisors were company employees (nonunion) and I was an elected shop steward in the IUE union and served as the executive board member at large. One could not be a supervisor and union official at the same time. The company had to create a job description for me and the union had to go along with the unique designation in the contract of agreement. When decision time came for me to go to the WELS ministerial training school in New Ulm, Minnesota the company did not want me to leave. They generously gave me a leave of absence with salary increments and vacations intact, as an enticement to return after one year. Surely God had a hand in that kind treatment given to a union official. This offer really helped because after my first year of school in New Ulm, I returned to Detroit to work all summer during the "Eisenhower Depression."

The Role of Faith

In New Ulm my first step was to finish high school. DMLC had a prep department on its campus in those days. Yet this presented a challenge for me. I had never read Luther's *Small Catechism*, let alone memorized the Chief Parts and it had been five years since attending school. The faculty at DMLC bent over backwards to help me achieve my goal. They doubled my religion classes that first year, which included memorizing Luther's Catechism, taught me geometry during the lunch hour, and arranged my gym classes with the older college students. Another challenge for me was making ends meet with the lost of a comfortable weekly income. So, my car, bowling ball and hunting stuff were sold for expenses. The road from Detroit to New Ulm was a long one, especially in the days before the interstate highways. Often hitchhiking became my mode of transportation to save the bus or train fare. One of my favorite Bible passages helped sustain me: "I can do all things through Christ who strengthens me." Everything worked out: AAL gave me an academic scholarship and I worked part time with the midnight shift in the sanitation department at the New Ulm Kraft Food Plant. The faculty and student body at DMLC accepted me and treated me well. An older student dressed in Detroit style clothes, must have stood out, but at this school an "outsider" could be an integrated part of a community of believers.

God's Blessings Though the WELS

I graduated from high school ("prep") and then Dr. Martin Luther College. Later I enrolled in graduate school programs at UWM and TCU. My first call I was privileged to serve as a principal and teacher at St. Paul's Lutheran in Franklin, Wisconsin (1959-1970). The second call I was honored become a college history professor at New Ulm, Minnesota: DMLC (1971 to 1995) and the amalgamated college MLC (1995 to 1998).

Becoming a WELS member turned my life around. Not everyone has a positive image of this conservative Biblically based church body, but those of us who have come to know her up close treasure her dearly. I will always appreciate what God through the WELS did for me and pray for its mission to be a blessing for others also.

Frederick Wulff

Book Review of Edwin S. Gaustad, *Sworn on the Altar of God: A Religious Biography of Thomas Jefferson* (Eerdmans, 1996) in *Lutheran Libraries*, volume 38, number 4, Fall, 1996

Edwin Gaustad has successfully presented the religious side of Thomas Jefferson. To help us understand this perspective of Jefferson, the author has carefully traced the evolution of Jefferson's religious development from his Anglican roots to his deistic theology of Enlightenment and finally to his reactions to the Second Great Awakening. We are shown how Jefferson's religious concerns permeated both his private and public life. Although Jefferson repudiated traditional Christian doctrine, Gaustad establishes the premise that Jefferson was profoundly religious in his outlook. This is accomplished by a scrutiny of Jefferson's "edited" Bible in which Gaustad carefully goes though the moral teachings Jefferson chose to preserve (in spite of the fact Jefferson deleted all references to miracles and the divinity of Christ). Further support of Gaustad's premise comes from his use of many written statements of Jefferson on religion, which expressed the same concern for moral principles. Finally Gaustad rather skillfully incorporates the private communications between Jefferson and his contemporaries, especially John Adams, James Madison, and Benjamin Rush, to shed even more light on Jefferson's personal theology.

This book could well serve clergy and laymen alike to review Jefferson's logical arguments for a wall of separation between church and state and the necessity for true religious freedom. In today's climate of secularism and immorality one could see why some church leaders would want to remove the wall and impose their brand of Christianity on society. Yet, this study of Jefferson helps us to critique that approach.

Another thought of Jefferson worthy of reflection in today's society is that democracy rests on freedom and requires responsibility. Gaustad notes that citizenship implies more than stress on the individual (in a private cocoon), but there is also stress, which relates to the community at large. He warns us of a multiculturalism (a group cocoon) that threatens national community by rejecting or ignoring common aspirations and a common morality. Liberty divorced from responsibility will result in a splintering of society. Jefferson preferred a society for all.

Professor Gaustad has written another scholarly book in church history. Sworn on the Altar of God is written in a clear and masterly style and worthy of a place in any library.

FHW

Book Review of Edwin S. Gaustad, *Neither King Nor Prelate: Religion and the New Nation 1776-1826* (Eerdmans, 1993) in *Lutheran Libraries*, volume 37, Number 1, Winter, 1994

Edwin Gaustad has written a concise book on an important chapter of church history in which he takes us back to the Founding Fathers who wrestled with church-state relations. This is done in such a way that we can better understand colonial religious perspectives and the struggle to escape imposed religious thought. The book could well serve as a guide for us today who still confront the tensions between personal religious freedom and public morality in the thorny issues of church-state relationships. The author's keen insights merit attention. Edwin Gaustad has gained wide respect for his scholarly writings on American church history and in this brief paperback has provided us with yet another well-documented work. The helpful appendix contains some of the major religious documents of the colonial period. The book is not only high on substance it is eminently readable. *Neither King Nor Prelate* could well serve clergy and lay people alike and would be a valuable addition to any church library.

(FW)

CHAPTER FIVE
COMMON SENSE AND MISCELLANOUS

CLEAN UP THE INCOGNITO MESS

A Letter to the New Ulm Journal, November 13, 2013

It is well that the Richie Incognito muck broke into the news. The NFL should come to grips with the "initiation" of freshmen football players. Actually, initiation is a euphemism for hazing that bullies can use to beat up or humiliate others. The practice creates a haven for misfits who enjoy hurting others. Judging from Incognito's past record he fits the definition of misfit. It should not be a badge of honor for Incognito to be called the dirtiest player in football. The victim Jonathan Martin was a second year player and he was still victimized, not only by Incognito but other players who left a dinner table to leave him sitting alone.

Vicious street gangs use hazing to instill loyalty to their membership and to desensitize members. This should not be accepted in the sports world even though defenders like Jared Allen maintain it sometimes has merit. Unfortunately, Geraldo Rivera recently commented that big adults should be able to "take it." Hurting other people either physically or mentally is assault. To force an individual to cough up $15,000 to pay for someone else's vacation is extortion. The social pressure to keep quiet or be labeled a sissy as one who can't take it is powerful. In a civilized society one should not to be placed in that situation. In another workplace setting this would rightly be called harassment.

Bullies in assault or extortion situations should be held accountable in a court of law. If Neanderthal coaches encourage such behavior to toughen up players, they should be fired without severance pay. Hopefully any investigations of the Dolphins will include the head coach and his coaching staff.

Both Minnesota head coaches Brad Childress and Leslie Frazier prohibited "initiations" as detrimental to the Vikings team spirit. Good football players do not need to be tough thugs. Reggie White who played for the Green Bay Packers did not have to be desensitized to be the force that he was. We need more responsible people like that in the sports world.

TRAVEL TO TUNISIA

A Letter to the Editor New Ulm Journal 2012 (printed as submitted)

Some travelers may have been apprehensive about visiting Tunisia in the aftermath of the January Revolution. My 15-day venture in May through that wonderful country encountered nothing that was stressful in any manner. I was so thankful I was not swayed away from an excellent tour in a country so rich in history and charm.

The people of Tunisia liked us Americans and they were very friendly. Excitement was everywhere from a newfound freedom of the press and the removal of a corrupt government. I was glad to help shore up their economy that is so dependent upon tourism.

COMMON SENSE AND MISCELLANOUS

The Muslims we encountered were moderate and had endorsed many Western ways. The population is young and savvy with modern communication methods. It was the young that brought about the Revolution in January. Actually, most modernization took place from 1956 to 1987 under Bourguiba (first modern president) who changed the lives of women in Tunisia. Before gaining independence from France in 1956, women were restricted to stay at home. He encouraged education, restricted arranged marriages, banned polygamy, and forbad the veiling of women at academic institutions. He called the veil an "odious rag" and regarded it as demeaning. His code set a minimum age of 17 for girls for marriage and gave them the right to refuse a proposed marriage. Currently, it is common to see women in any profession and very rare to see them veiled. 20% of parliament is reserved for women parliamentarians. The government requires parents to send girls to school, and today more than 50% of university students are women and 66% of judges and lawyers are women.

The leader of my tour, Mohamed Mastori, a devout Muslim, said that there was no way that the country could revert to past ways.

No site on our itinerary was curtailed because of any security threat

My primary interest as a former history teacher was the Carthaginian aspect of this country's story. It seemed as though Mohamed was almost apologetic that the ruins of the Punic period were not more in number, but I found so much rewarding in the ruins of Tophet, Byrsa Hill and the remains of Kerkouane. When we left Kerkouane I told Mohamed that the trip so far had already been worth the cost. The Roman ruins are an even greater attraction for many. Star War fans will appreciate the sites where the filming of the Star Wars movies took place. The country seems to offer everything. Probably the most memorable moment of the trip for me was being way out in the Sahara where we camped in tents. In the evening we sat among high sand dunes, drank wine under a star-studded sky and watched the colorful evening sunset. Oddly enough there were roaming camels in the wilderness that seemed oblivious to our presence.

The people of Tunisia really rely heavily upon tourism for employment. They need visitors to fill the hotels. I stayed at 5 star hotels where we (15 members) were the only guests. It is such a shame for people to miss this wonderful country and for Tunisians to languish because of misconceptions. Holland American Cruise Line continues to disembark passengers there. England has declared the country safe for its citizen to "holiday" there. Grand Circle Travel is only one of many companies that offer reasonable packages. Don't write off Tunisia. It is a gem.

BUREAUCRACY-ITIS

Originally written as an article for *The Lutheran Educator* in 2012
(but not submitted)

The Bad Image of Bureaucracies

Most people who hear the term bureaucracy cringe at the thought. The term often conjures up an image of a monstrous, bloated governing agency of non-elected officials. This sour reputation is not unique to our country. In fact, apprehension about a system of cumbersome office holders is quite universal. Jean Claude Marie Vincent de Gournay used to say, "We have an illness in France which bids fair to play havoc with us; this illness is called bureaumania." The Irish poet, William Allingham once said:

> Is it really necessary that men should consume so much of their bodily and mental energies in the machinery of civilized life? The world seems to me to do much of its toil for that which is not in any sense bread. Again, does not the latent feeling that

much of their striving is to no purpose tend to infuse large quantities of sham into men's work?

This poses the question: If bureaucracies are so universally criticized, how come they have been so firmly entrenched everywhere – even in the church?

The Roots of Bureaucracies

Bureaucracies go back at least to Imperial Rome and ancient China. From the beginning of the papacy, churchmen centralized administration to increase power and promote dependency. Historians contend that the growth of bureaucracies was one means by which secular rulers consolidated more effective power. Brandenburg-Prussia was transformed through the efforts of Frederick William, the Great Elector (1640-1688). He adopted all of Louis XIV's strategies to implement absolutist policies at the expense of the local notables.

Later, Frederick William III, under the pretext of an administrative reorganization, initiated the Prussian Union of 1817, which united Lutheran and Reformed churches and weakened the position of provincial churches. The state imposed merger of Lutheran and Reformed churches created problems for the conservative Christians who wanted to maintain distinctive Lutheran doctrine. Realizing the harmful consequences, some dissatisfied Lutherans in 1841 resisted this control and formed the Ev. Lutheran Church of Prussia which then became self-supporting and self-governing. Three years earlier, in 1838, confessional-minded Lutherans seeking doctrinal independence from the bureaucratic state church left for the United States and became the nucleus for the future Lutheran Church Missouri Synod.

Centralized governmental control was only one root cause for bureaucracies. Another major source for bureaucracies came with the

Industrial Revolution. In our modern industrialized society, bureaucracies became necessary, even indispensable, to large, complex enterprises. When organizations become large, there is a natural tendency for administrators to create commissions and offices to subdivide various functions into areas of specialties. Flow charts of authority, a listing of responsibilities and job descriptions, logically follow. This structuring makes sense according to the well-known sociologist Max Weber, one of the most influential users of the word in its social science sense. Weber, like the good German he was, believed that a permanent, well educated, conscientious, "nonpartisan," Prussian-style bureaucracy worked best. Weber described the ideal type bureaucracy in positive terms, considering it to be a more rational and efficient form of organization than the alternatives in feudal Europe and most other pre-modern societies (Max Weber, Essays in Sociology, Oxford University Press, reprinted 1948).

Bureaucracies as Good for the Church

Good? This heading may appear odd. There has been tension between bureaucratic systems and democratic principles throughout history. Among traditional Lutherans, who have been known to be fiercely independent, there is a tendency for us to stress local autonomy. The larger corporate body, or synod, could easily be seen as the "they" and viewed as separate and competitive from the "we" (individual congregations). Ideally, it would be better to see an "us" walking together as the working body of Christ. It is imperative that we build a cooperative and supportive relationship between our members and the larger church body to foster Christian fellowship and extend the Kingdom.

Obviously, there is much we must do jointly with other congregations that we cannot do alone. Such joint endeavors include supporting world missions, establishing Christian high schools, maintaining institutions for training church workers and helping those with special needs. In the case of our Wisconsin Synod, growth in membership and different forms of ministry has led to the establishment of centralized administrative offices and various boards. Understandably, we came to feel that more specialization was required for some positions and that a large church body would be better served by full-time office holders rather than part-time church workers with shared responsibilities. The motivation behind the trend towards bureaucracy was to do the best that we could do for Kingdom work. Yet, it behooves us to continually evaluate and fine-tune the machinery we have created, that it does not become something other than that which was originally intended.

Although Max Weber saw the need for large operations to incorporate a bureaucracy, he also emphasized that a bureaucracy had pitfalls. Utmost in our minds must be the question of how our church or our educational institutions avoid or minimize the pitfalls as we lengthen the cords and strengthen the stakes. We do well to examine some of these shortcomings lest we become too enamored by bureaucratic structure.

Pitfall #1 Inattention to Individual Cases

Bureaucracies may become ineffective when a decision must be adapted to an individual case. Usually a bureaucrat is responsible only for the impartial execution of assigned tasks. Max Weber wrote of the individual bureaucrat as only a single cog in an ever-moving mechanism. Impersonality may result at one time or another. We may have experienced dealing with a large company and been confused when we had to "choose from a menu of options" or were shunted from one desk to another because our particular problem did not fit any of its categories.

Bureaucrats need to keep a personal touch in administrative tasks. Perhaps those who are theologically trained could keep a foot in the preaching ministry by part time activities as guest pastors. Teacher trained faculty might fill limited teaching assignments. Such professional involvement could help prevent the malady known as "becoming institutionalized."

Pitfall #2: Stifling of Initiatives

Intentionally or unintentionally, bureaucracies can foster a stifling effect on individual initiatives of employees. Bureaucratic red tape can wear down even the most diligent workers or kill personal initiatives. A degree of freedom will have the opposite effect. When the writer of this article conducted American travel study tours for Dr. Martin Luther College, he really appreciated not being strangulated with rigid or complex procedures. Those who conducted the many European study tours would probably also concur in this opinion. Consequently, these popular tours were customized for instructional needs and the costs were kept exceedingly reasonable for students. Giving professors or employees more discretion, especially in their areas of specialty, may allow for much more to be accomplished.

Some administrative boundaries with clear rules and oversight are in order. It bodes well for an educational institution to grant the various departments academic dignity in making some decisions regarding course assignments, course offerings and course content. A wise policy in this respect will improve instruction and promote harmony between departments and the administration. The boundary and rules for elementary and middle school departments, if there is less specialization, will likely be more stringent; but still teachers should be given some discretion to be all that they can be. Wouldn't it be better to have general guidelines and limits that would still allow leeway for individualism, spontaneity and creativity?

Pitfall #3: Bureaucratic Growth

Those of us, who have an aversion to a myriad of full time-church office positions, are wary every time a new position is created. Many of these positions can be justified, but the number should be only in proportion to the numbers in the active preaching and teaching ministry -- lest we become top heavy. Excessive bureaucracy impacts the budget considerably. A prominent WELS speaker, announced at a recent conference (with tongue in cheek): "The Synod is having major financial problems, so we will hire a person to find out the reason." Questions arise. What impact does excessive administration and fundraising have on other essential programs? What proportion of our contributions actually goes into the programs that we intend to support?

Whenever there is an inclination to create a position, it might be well to first consider using volunteer workers or sharing responsibilities among existing staff. Maybe an ad hoc committee or special task force could suffice for an immediate or temporary problem. A "sunset" provision might be added to a commission so that positions could be eliminated when no longer needed. Sometimes bureaucracies take on a life of their own. Weber stated that once it is fully established, bureaucracy is among those social structures that are the hardest to destroy.

There may be some truth to Parkinson's Law whereby "work expands so as to fill the time available for its completion." The scientific observations, which contributed to the law's development, included noting that as Britain's overseas empire declined in importance, the number of employees at the Colonial Office increased. According to Parkinson, the total of those employed inside a bureaucracy rose by 5-7% per year irrespective of any variation in the amount of work (if any) to be done.

Pitfall #4 Inclination to Control

Many theorists believe that the people on the top of a bureaucratic ladder have a disproportionate amount of control. This seems logical. As stated earlier, the developments of centralized control both in the state and the Church of Rome grew out of bureaucratic settings. However, in Colonial America, many churches followed a Calvinistic trend of congregational authority. God does not prescribe what form of government the church must follow, but the congregational form is more democratic and suits well the concept of the universal priesthood of all believers. Our

SPEAKING OUT

Wisconsin Synod adopted this congregational type of organization that by theory has authority vested in the congregations, the broad base of the pyramid. Congregations then give direction to the elected Synod officials (via conventions) who then carry out their wishes. As for structure, or restructure, WELS president Karl Gurgel aptly puts it: "We have to keep in mind that proclaiming a living Jesus to a dying world is really the core of what we do and structure is merely a servant of our primary mission" (*Forward in Christ*, September, 2006. p. 22).

Synod's elected officials are aided by created agencies. Naturally, much influence is held by those officials who have specialized training and have honed their skills over years in performance of their duties. It is also only natural that some geographical areas of the synod or districts may have leaders of more influence than others. They set forth the needs or special interests of their constituents and use influence within the system to achieve those desired ends. However, budget considerations of Synod must take into account the various wish lists of others and priorities must be established. Organized lobbying or insider influence should not override the overall welfare and work of the Synod. The greater welfare should not be subordinated to parochial interests.

Within the bureaucracy of an educational institution, the same principle applies. It would be easy for a single department in a high school college to see its particular academic field as all-important and thereby harbor a limited mindset, rather than fully supporting the overall work being done by the other disciplines. It is imperative that a bureaucratic organization fosters the broader and more comprehensive goals of its mission.

In 2006 the 12 districts of Synod met for district conventions to discuss synod-wide matters prior to the 2007 Synod convention. Among the items was a synod-restructuring proposal (viewable on www.wels.net/jump/restructuring), which advocated creation of a National

Council. A number of districts passed resolutions opposing the proposal, some expressing concerns about the centralized decision making and reducing the check and balance system. (Forward in Christ. September, 2006, pp. 20-21). The November issue of *Forward in Christ* featured letters from readers who expressed reservations that administrators would make decisions rather than grass-roots –based boards (Feedback," *Forward in Christ*, November, 2006, p. 6). One could argue these are only perceptions, but perceptions are important.

Perceptions Within the Church

If church members perceive manipulation within a church body, cynicism may override the best interests of the Gospel ministry and apathy may follow. The perceptions our members have should not be dismissed easily. Even if the perceptions should be false, they become reality in that the consequences may be the same. The Synod has no enforcement power over individual congregations and has no taxing power to carry out assignments authorized by Synod conventions. Confidence in the system improves morale and cheerful participation.

Furthermore, if our members perceive that we have an overabundance of full time positions (vice-presidents, secretaries, assistants, coordinators, liaisons, councilors, directors, mentors, advisors, overseers, recruiters, planners, fundraisers or whatever we call them) that do not seem to have direct ties to the actual public ministry, members may become less enthusiastic supporting appeals for funding. The assignments under those labels listed above may be only for flow-chart purposes and may not actually be filled by full-time positions. If that is the case, this should be made transparent for fear that a false impression be given that we are supporting bloated administrative positions and office staff. Charities are often evaluated on the basis of percentages of donations actually used for charitable purposes over against administration and fundraising costs. Our members may make the same inferences.

SPEAKING OUT

In Conclusion

In times of budgetary restraints and the recalling of foreign missionaries, we might re-examine the growth of full-time administrators and related positions. Bureaucracy is necessary in a large complex organization, but because of the natural pitfalls previously discussed (and our Old Adam) it needs an occasional check-up and an awareness of public perceptions and relations. The final word is that organizational structure must serve the church and not be an end to itself. Be on the watch for the symptoms of "bureaucracy-itis" lest we become susceptible to the disease.

ENOUGH IS ENOUGH

Letter to the Editor submitted and printed
New Ulm *Journal*, October, 2011

I always look forward to reading your fine publication every morning. However, this morning I was disappointed to find a rehash or a rehash of a rehash of the Gibbon episode on the front page of the Journal. Not only was this rerun on the front page it dominated the front page. It appeared that you have an obsession with the lurid details of sexual abuse. This type of reporting is more in line with one what expects from the gossipy *National Enquirer*. I suggest you go back to what you do best – keeping the public informed with the latest news.

BOYCOTTING FOR "CHRISTMAS" IS ECONOMIC TERRORISM

Letter to the Editor November 25, 2013

I just received a e-mail from Monica Cole, Director of One Million Moms. She calls for a "Scrooge Alert" to boycott Radio Shack this

COMMON SENSE AND MISCELLANOUS

Christmas season because the company does not use the word Christmas in its advertisements. Ms Cole may be well meaning but I think she is ill advised. First of all I believe Christians should not coerce or force others to conform to her convictions. This is akin to those who would force other to close their businesses on Sunday because of their own personal viewpoint. Here in New Ulm we have a very fine Radio Shack that serves the community well. If Monica Cole wants to use economic terrorism, she should think of the collateral damage that takes place. Many Christians share ownership in Radio Shack and Radio Shack employs many Christians that would be hurt by a boycott. I personally lament the secularization of Christmas and like to use Christmas seals with a Nativity scene instead of puppies with red collars. I do not celebrate the "winter holiday" season, as much as I like snow. Putting Christ in Christmas is a personal matter. I do not think we have to resort to economic terrorism against those who think otherwise. Whether the national Radio Shack caves in to Monica Cole's threats or not, I will continue to do business with that company.